J
938
Nardo, Don

The Parthenon of Ancient Greece

The Parthenon of Ancient Greece

Don Nardo

San Diego, CA

© 2014 ReferencePoint Press, Inc.
Printed in the United States

For more information, contact:
ReferencePoint Press, Inc.
PO Box 27779
San Diego, CA 92198
www.ReferencePointPress.com

LIBRARY OF CONGRESS CATALOGING-IN-PUBLICATION DATA

Nardo, Don, 1947-
   [The Parthenon of ancient Greece (ReferencePoint Press)]
   The Parthenon of ancient Greece / by Don Nardo.
      pages cm. -- (History's great structures)
   Includes index.
   ISBN-13: 978-1-60152-538-3 (hardback)
   ISBN-10: 1-60152-538-9 (hardback)
   1. Parthenon (Athens, Greece)--Juvenile literature. 2. Athens (Greece)--Buildings, structures, etc.--Juvenile literature. I. Title.
   NA281.N375 2013
   726'.120809385--dc23
                                                                2012051717

CONTENTS

IMPORTANT EVENTS IN THE HISTORY OF THE PARTHENON

BC CA. 500–323

The years of Greece's Classical Age, in which Greek civilization reaches its political and cultural zenith.

447

Construction on the Parthenon begins.

404

At the close of the devastating Peloponnesian War, Athens surrenders and temporarily loses its cherished democracy.

BC **500**   **450**   **400**   AD **50**

480

A Persian army invades Greece, occupies Athens, and burns the existing temples on the Acropolis.

432

The Parthenon is completed.

AD CA. 46

The approximate date of the birth of Plutarch, the Greek writer who penned the most thorough ancient biography of Pericles, the Athenian statesman who directed the building of the Parthenon.

CA. 500s
Christian monks transform the Parthenon into a church.

2020
The projected date for the completion of the modern restoration of the Parthenon.

1990
An accurate copy of the giant statue that once stood in the Parthenon is added to the full-scale replica of the Parthenon in Nashville, Tennessee.

1833
After expelling the Turks, the Greeks begin restoration work on the Parthenon and other structures on the Acropolis.

1600   1700   1800   1900

1687
During a war between the Turks and Venetians, the Parthenon is struck by artillery fire and explodes, resulting in heavy damage.

1801
England's Lord Elgin begins removing large portions of the Parthenon's remaining sculptures and soon afterward sells them.

1975
The Greek government forms a committee to launch a major renovation of the Parthenon.

INTRODUCTION

An "Extraordinary Flowering of the Human Spirit"

n September 28, 1687, hundreds of Turkish soldiers and civilians, including numerous women and children, desperately tried to avoid the deadly cannonballs that rained down around them. Seeking safety, many of them huddled in or near a large ancient structure atop the Acropolis, the steep, rocky hill that rises near the center of Athens, Greece. The Turks, who then controlled Greece, did not know much about the history of the structure, known as the Parthenon. They did realize that it had been some sort of temple to the gods of the ancient Greeks. Moreover, the local Turkish rulers conceded, the building was handsomely decorated with well-carved bas-reliefs and other sculptures.

Yet there seemed no reason to see or treat the building, or any of the other old temples in Athens, as anything special. After all, the Turks were Muslims who believed in a single, all-powerful god, and in their eyes the ancients who worshipped multiple gods were misguided, or barbarous, or both. As a result, Turkish leaders had no concept that the ancient structures surrounding them might have any sort of historic importance or value. Thoughtlessly, they had recently placed a garrison, or military installation, on the Acropolis. They had also turned the Parthenon into a storage shed for their large supplies of gunpowder.

"Destroyed in a Moment"

These moves turned out to be a grave mistake. In 1687 the Turks found themselves at war with the Venetians (the residents of Venice, then a small but powerful independent kingdom). Late in September Venetian warships approached Athens's port town of Piraeus. Opening fire with their powerful cannons, they began bombarding the central portions of Athens, prompting Turks and Greeks alike to seek whatever refuge they could. Many of them hid inside the Parthenon, apparently assuming that its thick stone walls and rows of pillars would protect them.

That feeling of safety was an illusion, however. An estimated seven hundred cannonballs struck the Acropolis before one finally

Atop the Acropolis—the steep, rocky hill that rises in the center of Athens—stand the Parthenon and other structures dedicated to the city's patron goddess, Athena. The Parthenon's size and splendor have inspired people for centuries.

ignited the huge stores of gunpowder and other explosives stacked inside the Parthenon. "The dreadful effect of this," Cristoforo Ivanovich, an aide to the Venetian commander, later recalled, "was a raging fury of fire and exploding powder and grenades. And the thunderous roar of the said ammunition discharging shook all the houses around, even in the suburbs outside the [city's] walls."[1] The enormous blast instantly pulverized at least three hundred people. It also shattered the grand temple, which had remained largely intact for the twenty-one centuries since its creation, sending fragments flying in all directions.

Edward Dodwell, an English collector of rare antiquities (ancient artifacts) saw some of these pieces of the Parthenon still scattered about the Acropolis when he visited Athens almost a century and a half later. That the explosion had reduced the structure to a ruin overnight sickened and saddened him. After the disaster, he wrote in 1819, the thoughtless orgy of destruction continued, this time at the hands of the local Turks.

> Large masses of Pentelic marble were broken into smaller pieces for the construction of the miserable cottages of the garrison, while others, and particularly the bas-reliefs, were burnt into lime. For the Turks are said to have preferred for that purpose a sculptured rock to a plain one, though the material was the same. Such is the pleasure with which uncivilized ignorance or frantic superstition destroyed in a moment the works of years and the admiration of ages![2]

Western Culture's Founders

Many Europeans, Americans, and other Westerners who visited Athens in the 1800s were no less appalled by the deterioration of the Parthenon and its sister temples on the Acropolis. This was because they greatly appreciated the historical value of these structures. In the preceding two centuries, the Western world had come to realize that the ancient Greeks had laid much of its cultural foundation. They had bequeathed to later ages the concepts of democracy, philosophy, and the theater, along with a seemingly bottomless treasure chest of legal, political, literary, and artistic concepts. The latter included architectural styles that had come to be seen as noble and exceedingly attractive. Because Western architects wanted to copy those styles, they and other concerned individuals increasingly strove to rescue and preserve Greece's decaying ancient buildings.

In particular, foreign archaeologists and historians came to focus their attention on Athens. It became clear that that ancient city-state had been the most populous, wealthy, and culturally splendid in Greece. It had therefore produced an unusually large proportion of the finest Greek art and architecture. Greatest of all had been the magnificent complex of temples and other structures erected on the Acropolis during the Athenian golden age of the fifth century BC.

European and American historians came to call that pivotal period the Periclean Age, after Pericles, the dynamic statesman who led Athens to its height of power and influence in those years. Of all the Athenian politicians of his time, he lobbied the hardest to spend large portions of the city's funds on artistic projects. He urged his countrymen to create, in the words of his later Greek biographer Plutarch, "public works which, once completed, will bring [Athens] glory for all time."[3] Of these works, the one that Pericles pushed hardest for and that became his greatest achievement was the new temple complex atop the Acropolis. Thanks to him, the great sculptor Phidias, and other Athenians of extraordinary talent and vision, it would come to define and exemplify Athens in his own age and all of Greece in future ages.

An Unrivaled Triumph

That massive complex originally included a monumental gateway through which people walked onto the hill's summit; three temples, all dedicated to the city's patron goddess, Athena (the Temple of Athena Nike, the Erechtheum, and the Parthenon); shrines to other gods; altars for outdoor worship; and dozens of statues, some of them huge, of Athena and other deities.

Without a doubt, though, the hill's dominant feature, dwarfing all the others in size and splendor, was the Parthenon. Its towering columns, triangular gables, and chipped marble blocks created, and still create, a striking visual impression. Various visitors over the centuries have called it superb, heroic, miraculous, and awe-inspiring.

Even before people realized the building's importance to Western architecture, art, and culture in general, Europeans and other Westerners instinctively sensed that what they were seeing was special. The fifteenth-century Italian traveler Ciriaco d'Ancona left behind this description of the Parthenon after his 1436 visit to Athens, shortly before the Turkish occupation started:

> Inside the city and in the country round about I saw incredible marble buildings, houses, and sacred shrines, various works of figured sculpture conspicuous for their fine workmanship, and vast columns—all fallen in massive ruins. But what pleased me the most of all was the great and marvelous marble temple of the goddess Athena on the topmost citadel of the city, a divine work by Phidias, which has fifty-eight towering columns, each seven feet in diameter, and is splendidly adorned with the noblest images on all sides which you see superbly carved.[4]

Some four centuries later, Dodwell, who carefully measured the structure's contours, went further. He spoke of "the magnitude of its dimensions, the beauty of the materials," and "the exquisite perfection of its symmetry." Summing it up, he stated, "It is the most unrivalled triumph of sculpture and architecture that the world ever

Acropolis Site Plan with Major Archaeological Remains

1). Parthenon
2). Site of the Old Temple of Athena
3). Erechtheum
4). Statue of Athena Promachos
5). Propylaea
6). Temple of Athena Nike
7). Eleusinion
8). Sanctuary of Artemis Brauronia or Brauroneion
9). Chalkotheke
10). Pandroseion
11). Arrephorion
12). Altar of Athena
13). Sanctuary of Zeus Polieus
14). Sanctuary of Pandion
15). Odeon of Herodes Atticus
16). Stoa of Eumenes
17). Sanctuary of Asclepius or Asclepieion
18). Theatre of Dionysus Eleuthereus
19). Odeon of Pericles
20). Temenos of Dionysus Eleuthereus
21). Aglaureion

Source: Archaeography Photoblogging Collective, "Unpacking a Thing," A Map from 'Ten Things—Science, Technology and Design,'" February 23, 2006. traumwerk.stanford.edu.

saw."[5] Later still, in the twentieth century, the noted Swiss French architect Le Corbusier was no less overcome by the sight of the great temple. "One clear image will stand out in my mind forever," he said. It was "the Parthenon, stark, stripped, economical, violent, a clamorous outcry against a landscape of grace and terror."[6]

Preserved from the Touch of Time

Dodwell, Le Corbusier, and other modern individuals who witnessed the Parthenon in person recognized that no single attribute makes it great and important. Rather, it is a combination of factors. There is, of course, its sheer visual beauty and symmetry, even in a state of ruin, on which Dodwell commented. Others have pointed out that the Parthenon is the most prominent symbol of ancient Greek civilization, for which Americans, Europeans, and other Westerners maintain much fond admiration and nostalgia.

The great temple is also widely viewed as the finest example of precision and flawlessness in humanity's architectural annals. The words *perfect* and *perfection* have been used in connection with the Parthenon so often that they have become almost clichés. The late art historian Thomas Craven provided one of the most expressive examples. "From floor to gable and from end to end," he said, the structure "remains the closest thing to absolute perfection that art and handicraft have produced." He added, "To this day, architects, engineers and mathematicians hold conventions to discuss the scheme of proportions in the Parthenon and to try to discover the secrets of its perfection."[7]

No less crucial to the Parthenon's enduring appeal is its timeless quality. It fully served the Athenians' needs and aspirations when they erected it. Yet it also seems, almost magically, to transcend any single people, place, or time. This quality was plainly evident during Plutarch's lifetime, when the temple was more than five hundred years old—more than twice the age of the United States. Along with the other structures that Pericles and his colleagues erected on the Acropolis, Plutarch wrote, the Parthenon seemed to have been created not for a single society or age. Instead, it imparted to the viewer the idea that it had been constructed for *all* time. The very moment it sprang into being, he said, it already seemed "venerable," or impressive in its old age. And yet, it and the temples surrounding it conveyed "a youthful vigor which makes them appear to this day as if they were newly built. A bloom of eternal freshness hovers over these works of [Pericles] and preserves them from the touch of time, as if some unfading spirit of youth, some ageless vitality had been breathed into them."[8]

That special vitality remains as alive today as it was when Plutarch stood before the Parthenon, and well before, when the building first sprang from the hands and tools of Athenian artisans. Dozens of centuries of weathering, the 1687 explosion, and long ages of abuse and neglect have taken a toll, to be sure. But none of these have dulled what historian Peter Green calls "the extraordinary flowering of the human spirit" that created the temple and at the same time *is* the Parthenon. Its unique proportions and worn marble blocks are a kind of connection between present and past. By examining how the Parthenon was conceived and built, one can in a sense reach out to the ancient Greeks, who, as Green says, "still have the power to enthrall and quicken our understanding, from generation to generation, and for all time."[9]

CHAPTER ONE

The Rise of the Greek Temple

In 1838 popular American novelist James Fenimore Cooper put the following words into the mouth of one of the characters in his newest book, *Home as Found:* "The public sentiment just now runs almost exclusively and popularly into the Grecian school. We build little besides temples for our churches, our banks, our taverns, our court houses, and our dwellings. A friend of mine has just built a brewery on the model of the Temple of the Winds in Athens."[10]

Although the characters and plot of Cooper's novel were fictional, this little speech about American architecture in that era was not. It was Cooper's personal comment on the ongoing architectural movement known as Greek Revival. Hundreds of public and private buildings across the recently established United States copied the style of ancient Greek temple architecture.

Cooper himself had vivid memories of Greek Revival's beginnings in Philadelphia in 1801, when English architect Benjamin Latrobe completed the movement's first American building—the Bank of Pennsylvania. Latrobe borrowed heavily from temples erected during Greece's Classical Age (circa 500–323 BC), when Greek civilization and culture reached their height.

Cooper, Latrobe, and other educated individuals of their day marveled at Greek architecture, especially at what they viewed as the majestic form of temples like the Parthenon, on Athens's Acropolis.

The general thinking at that time was that Greece's Classical Age must have produced the most inventive and talented artists in history. Indeed, architects like Latrobe envisioned that the imposing style of the Parthenon and other Greek temples had sprung fully formed from the minds of the Classical Greeks.

The work of later archaeologists told a very different story, however. They found that the full-blown Greek temple style had evolved in an incremental manner, little by little over the course of hundreds of years. Furthermore, the ancestors of the Parthenon had been small, decidedly *un*imposing structures. An examination of these little edifices and how they eventually developed into a form that would influence architects for thousands of years is highly revealing. First, it shows the unique way that the Greeks viewed their relationship with their gods. It also shows how religious devotion and other factors made the Classical Age and Parthenon possible.

Hundreds of public and private buildings in the United States were built in the architectural style of the ancient Greek temples. This bank, in Pennsylvania, borrowed heavily from temples erected during Greece's Classical Age.

Bronze Age Shrines

Evidence indicates that the inhabitants of Greece were religiously devout for more than one thousand years before the advent of the Classical Age. However, the manner in which they expressed their spiritual feelings was not always the same. Building temples to demonstrate faith in and respect for the gods is a clear example. Early modern archaeologists assumed that there had always been temples in Greece, but this turned out not to be the case. In the late 1800s and early 1900s, excavators were surprised to find that even after architecture and the ability to erect large buildings had developed in Greece, for several centuries there were no formal temples.

The first of these large structures were palace-centers that arose on the island of Crete during Greece's Bronze Age (circa 3000–1150 BC). Modern experts use the term *palace-center* to denote that these sprawling, often multistoried buildings did more than house kings, queens, and other royalty. They also acted as distribution centers for food and other commodities used by the people who dwelled in villages surrounding the central structures.

⬡ TRANSITIONAL TEMPLES

The changeover from wooden to all-stone temples in Greece took more than a century. Between the mid-700s and early 500s BC, a number of transitional temples—using varied mixtures of materials—were erected. Not long after 600 BC, for instance, a temple dedicated to Hera was built in Olympia (in southwestern Greece). It had a heavy, tiled roof, and the first 3 feet (1 m) of the walls enclosing the *cella* (main inner chamber) were of stone. But the upper portions of the walls were made of less durable brick, and the columns were all wooden. Over time, the brick and wooden portions were replaced by stone. Similarly, the Temple of Poseidon at Corinth (west of Athens) and the Temple of Apollo at Thermon (in west-central Greece) began with wooden columns and entablatures and switched to sturdier stone versions later.

The civilization that created these palace-centers and villages on Crete was dubbed Minoan (after a mythical Greek king named Minos) by archaeologist Arthur Evans in the early 1900s. Evans and other scholars discovered that the Minoan kingdoms had no separate buildings used solely for worshipping the multiple gods they recognized. Instead, they paid their respects to these deities in what they saw as sacred places. These ranged from large caves, to mountaintops, to small shrines erected in tombs or in the palace-centers.

Meanwhile, the Greek mainland in the Bronze Age was occupied by people that historians called the Mycenaeans (after their fortress of Mycenae, in the southeastern part of the mainland). Athens was one of the chief Mycenaean towns, each the center of a small kingdom, and its local rulers maintained a small fortress-palace on the Acropolis. No significant remnants of that structure have survived. It appears that the town's central hill, whose name means "high place of the city," was also a religious center. But no evidence has been found for temples there or anywhere else on the mainland during the Bronze Age. Like the Minoans, whose culture strongly influenced them, the Mycenaeans worshipped at shrines in selected sacred spots.

A New Pantheon Emerges

These practices did not last, however, for Greek religion and worship underwent major alterations beginning sometime between 1200 and 1100 BC. During those years, the Minoan and Mycenaean kingdoms collapsed fairly rapidly for reasons that are still somewhat uncertain. The leading theory suggests that waves of well-armed invaders from southeastern Europe overwhelmed the mainland fortresses and island palace-centers. After much killing and plunder, the intruders moved on, leaving the region's survivors in a state of chaos and despair. Political systems, architecture, writing, and other aspects of advanced culture disappeared, and there ensued a long period of widespread poverty and illiteracy in which people largely forgot their heritage. Modern historians call it Greece's Dark Age, dating from about 1150 to about 800 BC.

Although the Greek lands had been devastated, all was not lost. In the widely separated, culturally backward villages that dotted the landscape, a new and in many ways different Greek culture slowly but steadily began to rise from the wreckage of the old one. By the 700s BC, the first century of the Archaic Age (circa 800–500 BC), prosperity had returned to Greece. Many of the little villages occupying isolated valleys and islands were growing into city-states. Each, consisting of a central town surrounded by outlying farms and villages, viewed itself as a tiny independent nation and fiercely guarded its territory and customs.

Although they were autonomous, these states shared a number of features of a common culture. First and foremost, they all spoke Greek and called themselves Hellenes. (They referred to their collective lands—what is now Greece—as Hellas.) Also, they recognized the same gods, several of them, to one degree or another, altered versions of the deities worshipped during the Bronze Age. The Greeks called that earlier era the Age of Heroes. Scattered memories of it survived in the Dark Age and emerged later in the form of myths about gods and human heroes who had sometimes interacted in the distant past.

Chief among these Panhellenic, or "all-Greek," divinities was Zeus, ruler of the gods, whose symbols were the thunderbolt and the eagle. His wife, Hera, was a protector of women and marriage, and his two brothers, Hades and Poseidon, ruled the Underworld and the seas, respectively. Meanwhile, Zeus's daughter, Athena, was goddess of wisdom and war. Her symbols—the olive tree and owl—were particularly important to the Athenians because she was their patron deity, or special protector. In addition to revering every member of the pantheon (a Greek word meaning "all the gods"), each city-state had its favorite, who became the local patron.

One way the people of each state paid their respects to their patron and other deities was by holding various festivals in their honor. These combined worship with parades, feasts, and other large-scale communal activities. In such celebrations, the late historian C.M. Bowra wrote, "a whole people might feel that it was protected by watchful presences and united in its admiration for them and its sense of belonging to them."[11]

Shelters for the Gods

As in the Bronze Age, the worship phase of the city-states' religious festivals took place in sacred spots, typically outside, where people

The ancient Greeks believed in many gods. Foremost among them were Zeus, king of the gods, and Hera, his wife, protector of women and marriage (both of whom are depicted in this painting).

erected stone altars. These holy places became known as sanctuaries. However, the emerging tradition in which independent national units recognized special divine patrons demanded the invention of a new way to honor those deities. It was thought that a community's patron frequently visited it so that he or she could more easily watch over and protect its residents. From that belief it naturally followed that the god required some sort of shelter or house to reside in while visiting.

This special, blessed structure, which began to emerge in the late Dark Age and early Archaic Age, became known as a temple. It was typically erected in an existing sanctuary, fairly close to its altar. Because people believed that the patron deity sometimes dwelled within the temple, it was imperative to respect that god's privacy. As a result, the custom evolved that no worship took place inside the structure, unlike with modern churches, synagogues, and mosques. The cella, or main chamber, of the interior of a Greek temple usually held a statue of the god or goddess—called his or her "cult image." (In Greece and other parts of the ancient world, a cult consisted of the collected beliefs, rituals, and myths relating to a given god.) A rear chamber of the temple was used to store the gifts worshippers brought in hopes of appeasing that deity.

WORDS IN CONTEXT

cella

The main room within a Greek-style temple.

The first temples in Greece were simple, plain-looking, hut-like structures. They were small—each about the size of a modern single-car garage, or even smaller. They were also composed almost entirely of natural, perishable materials, including wood, sun-dried mud bricks, bundled tree branches, and fieldstones. Because most of those materials deteriorate fairly quickly, none of these early temples have survived. However, archaeologists have discovered a few pottery models of these structures. One of them is believed to depict an eighth-century-BC temple built for Hera in Argos (in the southeastern mainland). The model shows a front porch with a triangular pediment, or gable, above the door. The pediment rests atop two thin, undecorated wooden columns.

ATHENA'S TEMPLES DESTROYED

The destruction of the temples and other sacred relics atop the Acropolis by the Persians in 480 BC was traumatic for the Athenians. The fifth-century-BC Greek historian Herodotus likely interviewed some surviving eyewitnesses of the event while compiling his famous historical work a few decades later. "The Persians found Athens itself abandoned," he wrote, "except for a few people in the Temple of Athena Polias." These individuals had "barricaded the Acropolis against the invaders with planks and timbers." The Persian troops laid siege to the hill and fired flaming arrows at the wooden barricades. This was only partially successful. So King Xerxes ordered a contingent of soldiers to climb up the steep, rocky walls rising along the sides of the hill. When the attackers made it to the top and began streaming onto the summit, Herodotus wrote, some of the defenders "leapt from the wall to their deaths, and others sought sanctuary in the inner shrine of the temple. But the Persians who had got up first made straight for the gates, flung them open, and slaughtered those in the sanctuary. Having left not one of them alive, they stripped the temple of its treasures and burned everything on the Acropolis."

Herodotus, *The Histories,* trans. Aubrey de Sélincourt. New York: Penguin, 2003, pp. 540–41.

In the years that followed, these few and simple components of the earliest temples increased in number and ornamentation as the structures themselves grew larger. One of the most important changes was the extension of the two front-porch columns into a colonnade, or row of columns, in the front. Also, designers often added a back porch. They gave it a colonnade of its own, and in time they included more columns running down the building's sides, eventually creating a pteron, a series of pillars that stretched around the entire temple. The first known temple of this kind in Greece appeared on the Aegean island of Samos in the early 700s BC. Dedicated to Hera, it was 106 feet (32 m) long and 21 feet (6 m) wide, and it had forty-three wooden columns in its pteron.

Other major alterations in temple design developed out of changes in roofing materials. Builders rapidly abandoned thatched roofs in favor of heavier, wooden ones, which in turn gave way to even heavier rows of thick pottery roofing tiles. In due course the traditional wooden columns and walls could no longer support all that weight. So architects decided to switch the wooden pillars and walls to stone. By the mid-500s BC, not long before the dawn of the Classical Age, the changeover to all-stone temples was complete across most of Greece.

Orders and Proportions

During that period of transition from wooden to stone temples, the earliest of the three orders, or styles, of Greek architecture came to be used in most of mainland Greece. It is called the Doric order. The two orders that developed later were the Ionic and Corinthian. As Thomas Craven pointed out, all three were most often distinguished by differences in the size, height, and capitals, or tops, of their columns. "This may, at first glance," he said, "appear to be an extremely elementary, if not insignificant measurement of styles. But the deviations between the three orders, the Doric, Ionic, and Corinthian, were carried from the structure of the column into every nook and cranny and proportion of the edifice."[12]

The shape of Doric columns illustrates this point. They stood directly on the temple's *stylobate*, or floor, without any sort of decorative base. That plainness, or lack of ornamentation, which architects refer to as severity, carried through to other stylistic features. The Doric capital, for instance, consisted of a flat stone slab resting directly on a simple rounded stone cushion. In almost all cases Doric columns were from five to seven times higher than they were wide, a ratio that gave them a somewhat sturdy or heavy look also seen as severe. In addition, each Doric column had twenty flutes, or narrow concave grooves, running vertically along its shaft.

Still another standard feature of the Doric temple was the distinct look of its entablature, the horizontal layer lying atop the columns and beneath the roof. Attached to that layer's outer surface was a frieze, or decorative painted or sculpted band, that was not continuous. It consisted instead of a series of separate square-shaped areas, or blocks, called triglyphs and metopes. Each triglyph contained three vertical bars, while each metope bore a painted or sculpted scene. These sculptures were done in relief; that is, they were partially raised from but still attached to the metope's flat surface. Meanwhile, the pediments resting above the structure's front and back porches were either blank or featured groupings of three-dimensional sculpted figures.

Not long after the Doric order appeared on the mainland, the Ionic order emerged in the Aegean Islands. It also developed in the Greek city-states located along the western coast of Asia Minor (now Turkey), an area then called Ionia, after which the style was named. In contrast to their Doric counterparts, Ionic columns had decorative bases, and their capitals bore elegant spiral scrolls called volutes. Also, Ionic columns were more slender and had a lighter look than Doric ones. Another important difference was that the Ionic frieze was typically a continuous band, without any triglyphs, that ran along the entablature on the building's front, back, and sides.

As would be true of the Corinthian style when it emerged later, the Doric and Ionic orders were primarily intended to make a temple or other building look beautiful. Over time, Greek architects recognized that a temple's basic proportions were also crucial. If the structure was too long or too wide, they realized, its beauty was diminished. A well-known example was the eighth-century-BC temple dedicated to Hera at Samos, which was five times longer than it was wide.

By the 500s BC the Greeks had come to view this and similar proportional ratios as awkward and unappealing. So architects decided on a new standard ratio of length to width—about two to one, which they all agreed best pleased the eye. Thereafter, with rare exceptions, builders adhered to it by placing six columns on each end of a temple and thirteen on each side (counting the corner columns twice).

Early Temples on the Acropolis

By 500 BC or so, at the start of the Classical Age, a number of all-stone temples employing the Doric order and the new two-to-one proportional ratio had been erected on the Greek mainland. Among the finest and most famous was the Temple of Athena Polias (Athena of the City), resting atop Athens's Acropolis. Its length was 100 Attic (or Athenian) feet, so it became known as the Hecatompedon, or "hundred-footer." (Using modern measurements, the building was about 110 feet, or 33.5 meters, long.) The structure's front pediment held a complicated array of statues that portrayed the Gigantomachy, or "war against the giants." It was the subject of a well-known Greek myth in which Athena and her fellow gods defeated a race of repulsive giants, a battle that came to represent the victory of civilization over barbarism.

The Athena Polias temple did not stand by itself atop the rocky Acropolis. Not far from it loomed an early version of the Erechtheum (or Erechtheion), also dedicated to Athena. Its name derived from Erechtheus, whom some scholars think may have been a Bronze Age Athenian king who passed into myth during the Dark Age, generating various legends. One portrayed him as a lesser deity associated with Athena, another as caretaker of her sanctuary in Athens, and still another as a large serpent that protected her. A succession of temples of uncertain style, all bearing the name Erechtheum, were built on the Acropolis before 500 BC, including the one that coexisted with the Doric temple honoring Athena Polias.

Other myths from Greece's Dark Age described the exploits of Erechtheus's divine master, Athena. Later, in the Classical Age, Athenian sculptors would depict excerpts from several of these tales by showing frozen moments from them in the sculptures in the Parthenon's pediments and metopes. One popular myth, for example, told how the goddess was born wearing the aegis, a splendid breastplate. In the words of the late seventh-century-BC Greek epic poet Hesiod, with that device "she surpassed in strength all her brother and sister gods. And Zeus brought her into the world,

Architecture on the Greek mainland was distinguished by three dominant styles of columns: (left to right) Corinthian, Ionic, and Doric. All were intended to create a sense of beauty in the structure.

ARCHITECTURE.

Plate II.

J. Ferry Jun.ʳ delin.

Lowry sculp.

London Published by Longman, Hurst, Rees & Orme, 1809.

bearing the aegis and clad in battle armor, from out of his head."[13] Another mythical tradition claimed that Athena threw an olive-wood statue of herself down onto the Acropolis, and the spot on which it landed became the site for the long succession of Erech-theum temples built on the hill.

The Potent Energies of Survival

In addition to the Temple of Athena Polias and the Erechtheum, dedicated to the local patron, the Acropolis of 500 BC featured other temples, as well as shrines to and statues of Zeus and various other deities. The Athenians saw them as their proudest possessions and expected them to last for centuries to come. But that particular future was not to be.

The fate of these relatively new and carefully constructed monuments to Greek religious devotion was in a sense sealed in the first decade of the Classical Age. In 499 BC the Ionian Greek city-states, then under the control of the huge Persian Empire (centered in what are now Iran and Iraq), rebelled. During the insurrection, the Athenians sent twenty warships to aid their fellow Greeks on the far side of the Aegean. Once ashore in Asia Minor, Athenian soldiers helped the Ionians burn Sardis, the capital of the local Persian province.

This bold act had dire consequences for all Greeks. The revolt failed, and once the Persian king, Darius I, had the Ionian cities back in his grasp, he sent an army to punish the Athenians for meddling in his affairs. Seeing them and other Greeks as barely civilized rabble dwelling on the outer fringes of the civilized world, he figured that subduing them would be a simple matter. So he was shocked when a considerably smaller force of Athenians crushed his army at Marathon, not far east of Athens, in 490 BC.

Enraged, Darius began preparations for a large-scale invasion of Greece. But he died soon afterward, and his son Xerxes ended up leading the assault. Some two hundred thousand strong and support-ed by hundreds of ships, the invasion force was the largest the world had yet seen. Like a giant steamroller, it pounded one Greek state after another until it reached Athens in September 480 BC. Xerxes was disappointed to find that most Athenians had fled, for he had looked forward to killing many of them and enslaving the rest. To vent his wrath, therefore, he destroyed their most prized possessions—the temples and shrines atop the Acropolis.

At that moment, the Persian monarch likely envisioned that he would soon be in control of all Greece. This was a grave miscalculation, however. Fighting for their homes and their way of life, the Athenians and other Greeks rebounded, routed the Persian fleet, and drove the invaders away. Then something both unexpected and vital to the future of Western civilization happened. The realization that a group of tiny city-states had soundly defeated the world's biggest empire instilled in the Greeks an enormous sense of achievement. "A dynamic spirit flooded all Greece," as historian John Crow puts it. The Greeks, and especially the Athenians, came to believe that "there was nothing they could not accomplish if they set their minds to it."[14] As a result, a series of events followed that no one could have predicted. The potent energies that had saved the Greeks from subjugation now propelled them forward into their most brilliant and creative age, in which they would produce their supreme achievement—the Parthenon.

WORDS IN CONTEXT
capital
The topmost section of a column.

CHAPTER TWO

The Planning and Structural Phases

In the years directly following the expulsion of the Persians from Greece, the temples, altars, and statues that had graced Athens's Acropolis lay ruined and blackened from the fires that had ravaged them. The inhabitants' initial instinct was to leave the wreckage as it was. Reportedly the Athenians swore the following oath in 479 BC, in the war's final days: "I will not rebuild a single one of the shrines which the barbarians have burnt and razed, but will allow them to remain for future generations as a memorial of the barbarians' impiety."[15] At first, therefore, no one expected that any new temples or shrines would be built on the Acropolis.

A generation later, in 449 BC, however, the Greeks and Persians signed a peace treaty. The men who now led Athens felt that this armistice at least partially released the Athenians from the oath sworn in 479. In addition, after the passage of three decades, Athens had become a much richer, stronger, and more influential place than it had been before the Persian invasion. The city had drawn together more than one hundred Greek city-states as allies who recognized it as their military adviser, leader, and protector. Moreover, these states paid yearly dues that were expected to help maintain their mutual military protection. However, the Athenians increasingly used portions of those dues to improve and beautify their own city, a practice many Greeks saw as inappropriate and arrogant.

So, although Athens itself was a democracy (having adopted that form of government in 508 BC), it had created a clearly undemocratic empire from which it continued to amass much wealth and prestige. All this gave the Athenians unbridled confidence in both themselves and the future. Moreover, to the leaders of their current generation, it seemed wasteful not to put their newfound wealth, power, and zeal to good use. That included clearing the unsightly rubble on the Acropolis. With astonishing energy and daring, therefore, in the decades that followed, the Athenians produced an outburst of political and cultural creativity the likes of which the world had never seen and would never see again. It included great works of philosophy and science; crucial innovations in painting, sculpture, and other visual arts; some of the finest plays ever written; and a new, splendid temple complex, including the majestic Parthenon, on the central hill.

The Persian army storms the Acropolis. Though the Persians were eventually forced out of Greece, the temples, altars, and statues that once graced the Acropolis lay in ruins after their departure.

To Attain Eternal Glory

The chief proponent of the new building program was Pericles. He had come to power in 461 BC in the capacity of one of the city's ten annually elected generals. These men were not only military leaders. They were also politicians who proposed new laws and statesmen who carried out the wishes of the Assembly, the democratic body of citizens that formulated the city's domestic and foreign policies. Pericles was seen as so smart and capable and was such a persuasive orator, that he was repeatedly reelected and came to overshadow most of his fellow generals.

Frequently, when addressing the Assembly in the early 440s BC, Pericles urged his countrymen to step up and realize their immense potential. Athens possessed talent and money in abundance, he said. Furthermore, the gods recognized the city as Greece's natural leader, a city that might attain eternal glory if only its own citizens had the same positive vision. "You must yourselves realize the power of Athens," Pericles told them, "and feast your eyes upon her from day to day, till love of her fills your hearts."[16]

The best way to fulfill Athens's singular destiny as Greece's leader, Pericles continued, was to pay homage to those same gods who had chosen it above all other cities. In particular, the Athenians should celebrate and glorify Athena, the goddess whose divine patronage had been a guiding force in the city's ongoing rise to prominence. The Persians had destroyed the lovely, comfortable houses that earlier Athenians had erected for her, Pericles said. If the present Athenians now utilized their formidable talent and money to build her some new and even grander temples, surely she would repay them with renewed guidance and protection.

Pericles also advocated that a stunning new assemblage of shrines on the Acropolis would make Athens the absolute envy of Greeks everywhere. It would symbolize and demonstrate Athenian greatness for generations to come and leave no doubt about why the city was fit to lead other Greeks. These arguments swayed the citizenry, and the Assembly approved the ambitious and grandiose new project.

⬡ THE GREATEST ATHENIAN STATESMAN

Much of what is known about Pericles comes from Plutarch's biography of him, penned in the first century AD. The following two passages tell how the greatest Athenian statesman pushed to expand the city's democracy in order to give the citizens more rights and enacted programs, including building projects, that would create more jobs and prosperity.

> [Pericles] chose this moment to hand over the reins of power to the people to a greater extent than ever before and deliberately shaped his policy to please them. He constantly provided public pageants, banquets, and processions in the city, entertaining the people like children with elegant pleasures.
>
> [He] raised the standards of the poorest classes, and by installing [military] garrisons among the allies, implanted at the same time a healthy fear of rebellion. But there was one measure above all which at once gave the greatest pleasure to the Athenians, adorned their city, and created amazement among the rest of mankind, and which is today the sole testimony that the tales of the ancient power and glory of Greece are no mere fables. By this I mean his construction of temples and public buildings.

Plutarch, "Life of Pericles," in *The Rise and Fall of Athens: Nine Greek Lives*, by Plutarch, trans. Ian Scott-Kilvert. New York: Penguin, 2011, pp. 176–77.

Because it was Pericles who sold the idea, the Parthenon and other structures built on the Acropolis in that period became forever associated with him. In this regard, the word *forever* was no overstatement. As Plutarch later pointed out, these buildings were not only exceedingly beautiful, but also built to last for countless centuries. "It is this, above all," he said, "which make Pericles' works an object of wonder to us—the fact that they were created in so short a span, and yet for all time."[17]

Layout and Themes

Once the new building project had been approved, decisions had to be made about exactly what structures would be created. There was also the question of how they would be laid out once the hill's summit had been cleared of debris. To answer these questions, Pericles sat down with other Athenian leaders, who likely included not only one or more of the other generals, but also a commission of citizens specially selected by the Assembly. It is possible that the main architect, Ictinus, and the chief sculptor and overall artistic director, Phidias, may also have been present to provide their valuable input in these important initial discussions.

Whoever was on this crucial committee along with Pericles, its members decided that the various temples and other components in the complex would be tied together by a few powerful conceptual and visual themes. It went without saying that the most essential of these themes was the city's patron, Athena. The committeemen envisioned that as visitors ascended the large-scale stone stairway that already existed on the hill's western side, they would see the first and smallest of her temples. Dedicated to Athena Nike (Athena the Victor), it would sit on a tall, separate platform protruding from the Acropolis's southwestern corner. Once the visitors had made it to the summit, they would catch sight of the bigger Erechtheum off to their left and the still larger Parthenon off to their right. Thus, no matter where a person stood on the Acropolis, he or she would be reminded that, although other gods were honored there, Athena was the primary recipient of worship.

Another theme that would be stressed throughout the new complex was the victory of civilization over barbarism. It would specifically commemorate the Greeks' triumph over the invading Persians, with an emphasis on Athens's role as a major leader in the conflict and thereby Greece's savior. But no actual Persians or other modern characters would be depicted. Instead, these things were to be portrayed symbolically, using the events and characters of famous myths. The defeat of the "barbarous" Persians, for example, would be represented by sculptures of the gods overcoming the savage mythical giants in the Gigantomachy. In addition, Peter Green explains, throughout the complex there would be visual images "calculated to remind a visitor of what Athena, and in an even greater sense Athens, stood for in moral terms—civilization, order, self-restraint, and creativity." In this way many of the sculptures of the Parthenon and other structures on the hill "were to provide visual propaganda, in the broadest sense of the term."[18]

Materials, Laborers, and Their Costs

After determining how the complex's general layout would look, the committee made some important stylistic decisions about the largest and most important structure that would rise on the hill—the Parthenon. First, Pericles and the others agreed that it would use the Doric order. They also concurred that both the Greeks of their time and people in future generations would judge the worth of Periclean Athens in large degree by the merits of this temple. So it needed to be as special and impressive as possible. One way they met that goal was by making it bigger than the standard Doric temple. Rather than six columns on each end and thirteen on each side, they gave it an arrangement of eight by seventeen columns, which still preserved the ideal visual ratio of roughly two to one.

Another way to ensure the temple's excellence was to use the finest materials available, no matter how expensive they might be. Fortunately for the builders, some of the best marble in all Greece existed in Attica, the large peninsula comprising Athenian territory. It was known as Pentelic marble because its quarry lay on a slope of Mount Pentelicon, situated about 10 miles (16 km) northeast of Athens's urban center.

Still, although the builders did not have to purchase the marble from another state, using it promised to be extremely expensive. This was partly due to the Parthenon's inordinate size. Because it would be longer, wider, and taller than an average temple, an enormous amount of marble would be needed—some 30,000 tons (27,215 metric tons) in all. Also, the hundreds, and at times thousands, of workers who would be quarrying, transporting, and stacking the marble blocks would have to be paid day after day, week after week, for several years. In addition, large amounts of high-quality, and therefore costly, wood, gold, ivory, and other materials would be required for accessories and decorations.

After examining surviving ancient written sources carefully, modern scholars have proposed a ballpark figure of 30 million drachmas for the Parthenon's total cost. Calculating how much that would be

Phidias, the Parthenon's chief sculptor and artistic director, brings stone to life in this fourteenth-century Italian relief. Phidias might have been one of the people who provided early input into the Parthenon project.

in today's money is close to impossible. But the spending power of the drachma in Pericles's time can be deduced by considering that an average Greek worker earned about one drachma a day, while a highly skilled artisan made two or three drachmas a day. So the Athenians who labored on the Parthenon each earned perhaps between 300 and 900 drachmas per year. Clearly, then, spending 30 million drachmas in a period of only a few years was a gigantic, quite unprecedented enterprise for a city of only one hundred thousand or so citizens.

Nevertheless, most of the voters in the Assembly enthusiastically approved the plans for the Parthenon. The general consensus was that though the project would be hugely expensive, it would also virtually abolish unemployment and thereby stimulate prosperity during the years of construction. The large array of jobs created—both skilled and unskilled—is known, thanks to Plutarch's account of the materials and workers in his biography of Pericles. "The materials to be used," he wrote,

> were stone, bronze, ivory, gold, ebony, and cypress-wood, while the arts or trades which wrought or fashioned them were those of carpenter, modeler, coppersmith, stone-mason, dyer, worker in gold and ivory, painter, embroiderer, and engraver, and besides these the carriers and suppliers of the materials, such as merchants, sailors, and pilots for the sea-borne traffic, and wagon-makers, trainers of draft-animals, and drivers for everything that came by land. There were also rope-makers, weavers, leatherworkers, road-builders, and miners. Each individual craft, like a general with an army under his separate command, had its own corps of unskilled laborers at its disposal [and] so through these various demands the city's prosperity was extended far and wide and shared among every age and condition in Athens.[19]

From Quarry to Worksite

After much talk and planning, the Athenians finally felt they were ready to begin the actual construction of the Parthenon in July 447 BC. Ictinus and another architect, Callicrates, whose exact role in the project remains unclear, put the first teams of laborers to work. Some prepared the area that would hold the structure's foundation, while others quarried marble blocks from Mount Pentelicon. To remove these blocks from the mountainside, the workers first employed mallets and chisels to cut grooves in the stone. Then they drove wooden wedges into the grooves and saturated the wedges with water. The wood slowly absorbed the water, which caused the wedges to expand, and in turn this created pressure that eventually made the marble crack and separate slightly from the hillside. The quarrymen finished this process by using crowbars and other tools to pry the stones loose.

After freeing the heavy blocks from the mountain, the builders faced the Herculean task of transporting them down the steep slope. Green briefly summarizes the way this was accomplished:

> The blocks had to be maneuvered on sleds down a paved quarry road (parts of which still survive), and only the smaller ones could be eased along on rollers. At intervals there were stout posts, carrying rope and tackle, which were used to help break the sleds' downward momentum. Accidents were not unknown, and one rough-dressed [stone], probably destined for the Parthenon, lies in a nearby ravine to this day.[20]

Next, the blocks had to be moved across 10 miles (16 km) of rugged plain and up the near vertical sides of the Acropolis. Some of these stones were so heavy that the builders greatly reinforced an existing

⬡ BUILT BY THE WHOLE COMMUNITY

Although Pericles was the chief instigator of the building program that produced the Parthenon, many other Athenians were involved to one degree or another. As the late, respected classical historian R.E. Wycherley put it:

> The Parthenon must have been the work of a committee. In a very real sense, it was the work of the whole Athenian people, not merely because hundreds of them had a hand in building it, but because the Assembly was ultimately responsible, confirmed appointments, and sanctioned and scrutinized the expenditure of every drachma. The Demos [people], besides having the first and last word, exercised control at every point, as in other enterprises, through the meeting of a board of commissioners, five in number, who saw to it that the plans were well laid and the money well spent.[1]

Another expert on the ancient Greeks, John Miliadis, agrees that the whole community created the Parthenon and points out that the project became an outlet for the stored-up talents and energies of thousands of creative, hardworking people. "It was not merely the passion for building," he says, "nor was it merely an exhibition of power. It was something deeper than all this. It was the irrepressible need of a whole generation which took the highest intellectual view of life, to find a creative self-expression."[2]

1. R.E. Wycherley, *The Stones of Athens*. Princeton, NJ: Princeton University Press, 1992, p. 113.
2. John Miliadis, *The Acropolis*. Athens: Pechlivanidis, p. 14.

road in order to support their bulk. Likewise, they constructed extra-large wagons with wheels 12 feet (3.7 m) across and gathered an unprecedented sixty oxen to pull each wagon. When such a wagon reached the base of the Acropolis, a specially trained gang of workers hefted the stone onto a huge sled, attached numerous ropes to the sled, and with the aid of more oxen on the summit, dragged it up the hillside. To move a single stone from the quarry to the worksite consumed at least two days and the energies of dozens of people and animals.

Preparing and Stacking the Stones

As the rough-hewn marble slabs arrived atop the Acropolis, teams of stonemasons went to work on them. They used flat chisels, which they struck with heavy wooden mallets, to cut and trim each block so it would fit into a spot that the architects had already premeasured. This work had to be accomplished with tremendous precision because no mortar was used to bind the stones to one another. Rather, after a block was in place, workers joined it to its immediate neighbors using I-shaped iron clamps that were ingeniously hidden from view.

To install a clamp, the workers chiseled rectangular niches in the upper surfaces at the sides of two adjacent blocks. Then they inserted the clamp so that half of it lay in one niche and half in the other. The next step was to pour melted lead into the spaces that remained around the clamp in such a way that the surface of the hardened lead would be even with the surfaces of the two blocks. Finally, the workers laid the next course of marble blocks on top. These higher stones conveniently covered and concealed the clamps in the course below.

While some teams of workers continued to lay the rectangular-shaped stones making up the temple's walls, others prepared the rounded blocks that made up the massive columns. These circular stones were called drums. Greek builders stacked several drums to form a column. In the Parthenon, which had bigger columns than standard Greeks temples, each column was made up of eleven separate drums, to which was added a Doric capital on top.

When a mason was ready to prepare a still rough-hewn drum, he placed it on top of a circular stone pattern resting on the ground. Taking hold of a mallet and a pointed metal tool (fittingly referred to as a *point*), he started chipping away portions of the drum until its size matched that of the pattern beneath it. The pattern was a little less than 2 inches (5 cm) wider than the finished column would be. This gave the mason a little extra thickness of stone in which to carve the flutes, a task he would tackle later, when most of the major construction work was finished. Builders knew from experience that dropped tools and other normal minor accidents that occurred on worksites could damage the flutes' delicate edges.

Workers joined the column drums with metal clamps much like the ones used to keep the wall blocks in place. The masons carved out a rectangular slot in the center of the top and bottom surfaces of each drum. Then carpenters inserted wooden plugs into the notches and employed hand-turned drills, called augers, to bore holes in the centers of the plugs. Lastly, they put rounded wooden pins inside the holes. That way, when the drums were stacked, the pins kept them precisely centered above one another. The clamp and pin in a drum's top surface were hidden by the drum stacked above, just as a wall block concealed the clamp that joined the two blocks below it.

Simple but Ingenious Hoists

It is important to emphasize that the stacking of the wall blocks and column drums was impossible to do by hand because of the extraordinary weight of these stones. For example, modern experts have calculated that each of the Parthenon's column drums weighed an average of 7.5 tons (6.8 metric tons), equivalent to more than three average modern automobiles. After multiplying that figure by eleven (because a column had eleven drums), one must add in the weight of the column capital, which averaged about 8.5 tons (7.7 metric tons). A single Parthenon column therefore tipped the scale at an amazing 91 tons (82.6 metric tons), about the weight of a large modern house. Considering that the temple had forty-eight outer

The Parthenon

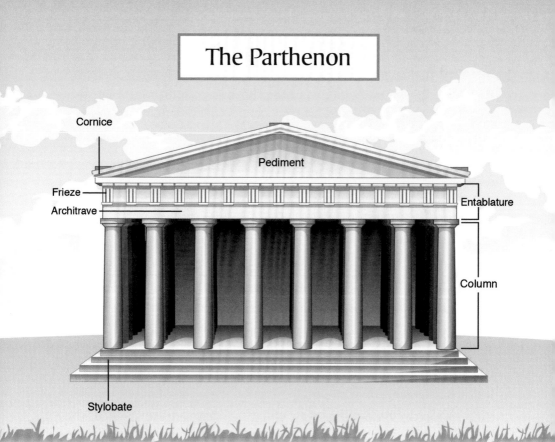

Cornice

Pediment

Frieze

Architrave

Entablature

Column

Stylobate

columns, the total weight of its pteron was approximately 4,368 tons (3,963 metric tons), the equivalent of forty-eight large houses.

Clearly, raising and maneuvering such phenomenally heavy objects, particularly the ones intended for the structure's upper portions, was enormously difficult for builders in preindustrial societies like that of the ancient Greeks. They lacked advanced lifting devices like today's steam cranes and backhoes. So they used simple but ingenious and surprisingly effective mechanical hoists. The most common kind was equipped with a system of pulleys, which were attached to a wall block or drum in one of several ways. As archaeologist Lesley Adkins explains:

> Holes were sometimes drilled in the top of the block. For example, ropes would be passed through U-shaped holes or attached to a lewis iron wedged into lewis holes with pack-

ing materials. A lewis iron was an iron plug shaped like half a dovetail, with the bottom end wider than the top. Similar holes could also enable lifting tongs to achieve a grip. In some cases, projecting pieces of stone [called bosses] were left on the sides of the block to help secure a sling for lifting. They were usually removed after the block was built into the wall, but some walls still have these handling bosses in place.[21]

Once a hoist had lifted a block into its preplanned spot, workers used crowbars to jostle it into its exact position. Two, three, or more hoists, each with its own crew of masons and laborers, were likely in use simultaneously at any given time during the Parthenon's early construction phase. It was during that period, lasting perhaps five to six years, that the building's superstructure—consisting of its base, walls, columns, and still-empty pediments—was completed.

Pericles's Master Plan

By today's standards, particularly considering that the temple was still largely an empty, unadorned shell, this seems like a long time. Yet ancient peoples were used to construction periods of a few years for large buildings. It should also be noted that Phidias and his assistants were already carving statues for the pediments and relief sculptures for the metopes. Attaching these artistic elements to the superstructure would be part of the second major phase of construction.

WORDS IN CONTEXT
hoist
A mechanical lifting device.

Although there is no way to know for sure, it is possible that over the years a number of Athenians grew tired of seeing the urban center's streets choked with giant wagons coming and going. The incessant clamor of mason's hammers and other construction noises may also have become wearisome to some. More certain is that the farsighted Pericles was in no hurry to see the Parthenon completed.

According to Plutarch, he was glad to see a large percentage of the populace gainfully employed, financially secure, and working to benefit both themselves and their homeland. Plutarch wrote that it had been part of Pericles's master plan all along to create a community-wide project "which would involve many different arts and industries and require long periods to complete, his object being that those who stayed at home, no less than those serving in the fleet or the army, should be enabled to enjoy a share of the national wealth."[22] This and other ancient evidence shows the distinctly democratic circumstances under which the Parthenon was conceived. Of history's best national leaders, few sought to increase the well-being and happiness of the people they guided as sincerely and selflessly as Pericles did.

CHAPTER THREE

Decorations to Please the Gods

Not long after the Parthenon's superstructure was completed in the late 440s BC, Phidias and his assistants began to add the sculptures and other decorations they had already finished. It is important to emphasize that although the great artist probably designed all of the temple's sculptures, he did not carve them all by himself, as implied in some modern books. Indeed, author and historian Mary Beard points out, "he could not possibly have had the time to lay his chisel on more than a tiny proportion of the marble. Huge numbers of trained sculptors would have been needed to get through the work on what was clearly a tight schedule. On the Ionic frieze, for example, as many as eighty different hands have been detected."[23]

These helpers and their boss had been hard at work producing their first batch of sculptures throughout the period in which the walls and columns were rising. This finely detailed work of carving human and animal figures was done mostly in temporary workshops set up on the Acropolis's summit. Even as some of Phidias's teams were installing the initial reliefs and ornaments, others started work on those that would be mounted on the building in the months and years to come.

A Gathering of Forces

Most of these embellishments the artisans added to the basic structural elements did not appear off-white, or plain and colorless, as they do today. Early modern visitors, including archaeologists and other scholars, assumed the decorations *were* originally colorless. Moreover, they came to feel that the overall plain marble look of the ruins was somehow aesthetically, or artistically, beautiful and noble looking.

It came as somewhat of a shock and disappointment for some moderns, therefore, when archaeologists discovered that the building was initially alive with bright colors. Scholar John Miliadis elaborates, explaining that

> the upper parts of the building, which caught the strongest light, were coated with strong colors that could withstand the out-of-doors: deep red, blue, and here and there black and gold. The coloring, however, was not general, nor was it without reason. The chief architectural features, those with a constructive purpose, received no color. Color was reserved for the secondary parts. Thus, apart from the variety contributed by the color, it further emphasized the force of the main lines of construction.[24]

The structure's decorative elements were much more than merely visually impressive and pleasing, however. In their design and presentation, especially in the way they mixed Doric and Ionic concepts, they were highly innovative and groundbreaking and would strongly influence later Greek, Roman, medieval, and modern architecture. The Parthenon's artistic touches, historian Vincent J. Bruno points out, had

> the character of a gathering of forces, a work in which the most important developments of fifth-century B.C. Greek art were embodied and given for the first time a clear and unequivocal statement. The result was a new understanding of the possibil-

ities inherent in such a work, and this in turn produced a series of changes that could only end in infinite variety—the variety of artistic modes of expression that, indeed, characterized the later periods of antiquity. The designers of the Parthenon gave definition to a new concept of art, [one] that contained the seeds for many of the forms of artistic expression mankind has witnessed in more recent periods.[25]

Work on the Entablature Begins

A large proportion of the sculptures and other decorations designed by Phidias were destined to adorn the entablature. Because that horizontal band rested above the towering columns, work on it, as well as on the roof itself, required the use of scaffolding. The version of scaffolding employed in ancient Greece consisted of a sturdy framework made of wooden poles lashed together at the joints and corners by ropes. The workers stood on wooden boards resting flat on appropriate areas of the framework.

Because the wood and ropes used in Greek scaffolding rotted away long ago, no traces of these frameworks that were so vital to large-scale construction have survived. Modern experts know what they looked like, however, because a Greek artist depicted part of one on an elegant drinking cup discovered in 1837. Dubbed the Berlin Foundry Cup (because it is on display in a museum in Berlin, Germany), it dates from sometime between 490 and 480 BC. Among the cup's several exquisite renderings of fifth-century-BC artisans at work is one showing bronze workers polishing a larger-than-life statue of a warrior. The statue is encased by a large section of scaffolding.

Such a framework was securely in place when Phidias began working on the Parthenon's Doric frieze. By the time the temple was conceived, the Doric order had developed a standard ratio of entablature height to column height. It was one to three, meaning that the entablature's thickness was one-third the height of a column (and conversely, a Doric column was three times taller than the height of a Doric entablature).

The entablature's lower section was the architrave (or epistyle). Structurally speaking, it was a brace or beam resting atop the pteron and supporting the temple's upper portions. The architrave was made up of a long row of large, rectangular stone blocks placed in such a

This portion of the Parthenon's splendid Ionic frieze presently resides in an Athens museum. It shows some of the horsemen—probably members of noble Athenian families—who rode in the grand religious procession that annually honored Athena.

way that the seam formed where two blocks met rested directly above the center of one of the columns below.

As a rule, the architrave itself was left undecorated. But right above it, and approximately equal to it in depth, was the highly ornamented Doric frieze, with its alternating triglyphs and metopes. Phidias had his workers space the triglyphs, each featuring a cluster of three vertical stone bars, so that they followed the existing rules of Doric architecture. This spacing allowed for fourteen metopes on each end of the building and thirty-two on each side, for a total of ninety-two metopes.

WORDS IN CONTEXT
architrave
The lower section of the horizontal layer lying atop the columns and beneath the roof of the temple.

Four Versions of Order over Chaos

One of the first jobs executed by Phidias's team was to attach the already prepared relief sculptures to the metopes' flat surfaces. The scenes depicted in these reliefs were typically elegant but fairly simple in composition, with only two or three figures in each. Those figures were based on humans and/or creatures from mythology. Like many other sculptures on the Parthenon's outer and inner surfaces, they personified the theme of the Greek, and particularly the Athenian, victory over the forces of chaos and savagery.

In fact, the temple's ninety-two metopes contained four separate versions of that theme. The metopes on the building's northern side, for instance, displayed well-known events from the Trojan War. The Athenians had come to see that conflict from their dimly remembered past as a forerunner of the recent war between the Persian invaders and Greek defenders. In a larger sense they also viewed it as the triumph of the supposedly civilized and rational West over the unenlightened and sinister East, or more concisely Europe over Asia. This unapologetic Eurocentric theme was destined to haunt both Greek and Western art for centuries to come.

Meanwhile, the metope scenes on the Parthenon's eastern side showed another example of civilization overcoming barbarism. In this case it consisted of episodes from the Gigantomachy, the legendary battle between the giants and Olympian gods. Similarly, the metopes on the temple's western side portrayed scenes from another famous mythical fight between civilized Greeks and vulgar outsiders—the Amazonomachy. Deriving from the Age of Heroes, it was the war in which the Athenians defeated the invading Amazons. In the myth, this race of warrior women had assaulted Athenian territory at Marathon, just as the Persians had in real life.

The metopes on the Parthenon's southern side bore sculptures depicting still another mythical clash between culture and crudity. Known to the Greeks as the Centauromachy, it featured the Lapiths, members of an early Greek tribe, battling Centaurs, legendary creatures said to have been half human and half horse. "The bestial Centaurs were forces of disruption," archaeologist Nigel Spivey writes, "threats to the order and civilized sanctity of Greek institutions."[26]

One way that Phidias made the thematic connection between the disruptive Centaurs and equally disorderly Persians was to show the Centaurs fighting with uprooted trees. Greeks who saw this image immediately understood that it represented the deliberate destruction of olive trees by Persian soldiers when they occupied Attica during the invasion of 480 BC. "The association of the Persians with Centaurs reduced them to the level of animals," Spivey explains. Such scenes in the temple's metopes, he adds, "may be read as being invested with a mythical symbolism that exalted Greek or Athenian order over those who would challenge it."[27]

The Cornice and Roof

Once the Doric frieze had been completed, one of Phidias's teams added the entablature's uppermost segment. Called the cornice, it was made up of several separate parts, the lowest of which was a horizontal stone beam or ledge that projected outward, overhanging the frieze below by a bit more than 2 feet (61 cm). Along the underside of this ledge, facing downward, the artisans attached an array of rectangular, plaque-like decorations called mutules. A single mutule hung above each triglyph, as well as above each metope. In addition, there was a mutule situated under each of the temple's four corners, which meant the total number of mutules on the structure was 188. Also, the underside of each mutule had eighteen rounded stone pegs, called guttae, that projected slightly downward. Some Americans who have visited the Parthenon have pointed out that the mutules, with their rows of pegs sticking out, look remarkably like Lego plastic building blocks.

The mutules and guttae were nods to architectural tradition. Back in the era in which Greek temples had been made of wood, builders had secured the roof to the cornice with wooden fittings.

⬡ ALTERNATE THEORIES OF THE IONIC FRIEZE

Most archaeologists and other modern scholars think that the Parthenon's Ionic frieze depicted the grand procession staged during the Greater Panathenaea. Athens's biggest and most important religious festival, it was staged every four years. A few experts have expressed doubts about that explanation of the frieze, however. One alternative theory proposes that the scene of marching animals and humans came from a myth about Erechtheus, the early Athenian king later seen as Athena's partner or protector. In that tale, the gods advised Erechtheus to sacrifice his daughter in order to stop an enemy attack. In this view, the marchers in the frieze were Erechtheus, his family members, and their horsemen and attendants, who were getting ready for the sacrifice while several gods watched them. A third interpretation of the procession seen in the frieze suggests that it celebrated the victory over the Persians at Marathon. There were 192 horsemen in the frieze, this theory claims, who represented the 192 Athenians who died in the battle.

Each fitting was a rectangular board pierced by eighteen nails whose back ends were allowed to project slightly from the board. People got used to seeing these fittings as part of the overall look of a temple. So when stone temples replaced wooden ones, architects retained nonfunctional stone representations of those boards and nails—the mutules and guttae. (In the Parthenon the mutules were joined to the cornice by hidden metal clamps like the ones used in the column drums and wall blocks.)

WORDS IN CONTEXT

cornice
The uppermost section of a temple's entablature.

Installing the cornice above the entablature required the use of a framework of scaffolding that almost certainly encased all of the lower portions of the unfinished temple. That scaffolding remained in place for as long as it took to construct the building's massive roof. To install the roof, workers first laid enormous wooden timbers atop the inner walls and outer entablature just behind the cornice. Those timbers acted as the main supports for a complex assemblage of crossbeams and rafters that, in turn, held up the tremendously heavy pottery roofing tiles. In this manner the architect and builders distributed the roof's weight fairly evenly across numerous vertical supports, or piers. Because the piers (the walls and columns) were made of stone and very thick, they were exceedingly strong. This was a must, considering that the combined weight of the roof's timbers, rafters, and tiles was an estimated 3,000 tons (2,722 metric tons).

A majority of the roofing tiles were Corinthian in style. Each featured two flat ceramic pieces enclosed and connected by a triangular ridge. That triangular shape caused rainwater to trickle sideways and downward. To dispose of the water, the late A.W. Lawrence, an expert on Greek temples, wrote,

a raking [slanting] gutter was provided on the ends of the building and along the side. This was formed, when using pottery tiles, by turning their edges upwards. The ends of the raking gutter were usually turned for a short distance along

the sides, emptying through a spout—preferably in the shape
of lion heads with open mouths. The aim was to ensure that
rainwater was thrown well clear of the walls.[28]

The Pedimental Scenes

When the roof was completed, much of the scaffolding was removed
from the temple's sides. But the portions of scaffolding mounted
along the front and back porches had to stay in place so that the
sculptors could install the pedimental figures. These magnificent,
larger-than-life statues began as small clay models resting within a
miniature pediment in Phidias's workshop. There, he experimented
with the general look of the shapes and proportions of the figures
and scenes until he, and perhaps the committee overseeing the project, was satisfied.

Next, a full-scale clay model of each figure was fashioned. Phidias's assistants modeled most of these, although it is likely that, as
noted scholar John Boardman suggests, "the master intervened at every stage to check pose and proportions."[29] When Phidias, and again
maybe those who outranked him, felt the clay versions were just right,
the sculptors copied them in stone, using the standard tools of that
work both then and now—chisels, mallets, and hand drills.

When the basic stone carving was finished, the sculptors stepped
back and allowed other craftsmen to take over. Bronze workers af-
fixed premade metal horse harnesses, spears, and other such accessories to holes the sculptors had already drilled. Then teams of
painters applied wax to the surfaces representing human skin. They
also painted the lips, hair, and eyebrows of the human figures a deep
red and the clothing of the carved bodies assorted shades of blue,
red, and yellow. The craftsmen were even careful to accessorize and
paint the statues' backs, which would not be visible to anyone after
they had been mounted on the temple. They believed that "what the
human eye might miss, the divine might criticize,"[30] as Boardman
phrases it.

PAUSANIAS DESCRIBES THE ATHENA PARTHENOS

The Greek traveler Pausanias, who hailed from Ionia, in Asia Minor, spent fourteen years—from the late 150s to early 170s AD—touring the Greek mainland. He left behind a guidebook describing the places he visited. This passage from the book describes Phidias's enormous statue of Athena that stood in the Parthenon's cella:

> The statue is made of ivory and gold. She has a sphinx [monster with a woman's face] on the middle of her helmet and griffins worked on either side of it. . . . The griffins are wild monsters like lions with wings and the beak of an eagle. This is enough about the griffins. The statue of Athena stands upright in an ankle-length tunic with the head of [the hideous monster] Medusa carved in ivory on her breast. She has a [statue of] Victory about eight feet high, and a spear in her hand and a shield at her feet, and a snake beside the shield. This snake might be Erechtheus. The plinth [platform] of the statue is carved with [a scene showing] the birth of Pandora. [The Greek epic poet] Hesiod and others say Pandora was the first woman ever born, and the female sex did not exist before her birth.

Pausanias, *Guide to Greece*, vol. 1, trans. Peter Levi. New York: Penguin, 1984, pp. 69–70.

Finally, after the stone versions of the figures were ready, they were attached to hoists and lifted upward for installation inside the pediments. Each of the two scenes they formed (one in the front pediment, the other in the rear pediment) contained roughly twenty-two principal figures and portrayed a major myth associated with the city's divine patron, Athena. The western pediment displayed the competition between her and her uncle, Poseidon, to see which of them would represent Athens. The eastern pediment showed Athena's spectacular birth from her father's head, with other divinities looking on in amazement.

Creation of the Ionic Frieze

No less amazed were the Greeks and foreigners alike who gazed on the finished pedimental scenes and marveled at the sheer artistry displayed by Phidias and his helpers. Yet these sculptors had, in the opinion of many modern experts, saved the proverbial best for last. In this view, the Parthenon's artistic masterpiece was the second frieze, which ran directly behind and parallel to the Doric frieze. Because the inner-facing frieze was Ionic, it had no triglyphs. So it consisted of an unbroken band of reliefs that extended about 524 feet (160 m) around the entire building.

One major difference between the two friezes was that the Ionic one was carved *in situ*, or in place, rather than done in pieces in a workshop and later attached to the temple. To achieve this extraordinary feat, the sculptors erected some scaffolding in the narrow walkway located between the pteron and walls. They stood or knelt in a confined space more than 30 feet (9 m) above the walkway. Tucked behind the entablature where it was poorly lit, they had to use lamps (that burned olive oil) and torches to illuminate the work.

Even after the frieze was completed, its partly concealed position and the lack of natural lighting in that area made it very difficult to see from the walkway, even when a viewer stood with his or her back to the wall blocks. Beginning in the 1700s scholars and other observers in succeeding generations found this arrangement odd. Why, they typically asked, did the builders put this imposing piece of artwork in a place where few people could see and appreciate its resplendent features? Today the consensus of historians is that the Ionic frieze was primarily a religious offering to Athena and perhaps other deities, too. As such, it was specifically aimed to please divine rather than human eyes.

Whomever it was meant to satisfy, the Ionic frieze was most likely a sculpted depiction of a major religious celebration held by the Athenian people to honor their divine patron. It showed a procession, or parade, that included dozens of men on horseback, followed by chariots and numerous citizens marching on foot. Among the latter were bearded elders, musicians, girls and others carrying trays of food for a great feast, people leading cattle and sheep toward a sacrificial altar, and many others representing every walk of life. All of the figures, humans and animals alike, were strikingly lifelike, giving the impression of a solemn yet festive moment in time caught in a sort of stone snapshot. "As we look at this frieze," Miliadis says, "we seem to hear a hymn of praise to the city that had such feasts, such citizens, such youth." Absent is any "exhibition of material power," he adds. Instead, "everywhere it is the spirit of the inner life of a noble people."[31]

Ideal Forms and Faces

With its friezes and pediments overflowing with sumptuous sculptures, its stately rows of towering columns, and its well-planned placement of hundreds of colorful decorations, the Parthenon's exterior was undoubtedly a superb sight. Pericles, Phidias, Ictinus, and the other planners aspired to make the temple's interior no less impressive. In this effort, according to the judgment of posterity, they succeeded admirably.

The cella was dominated by Athena's cult image. Known as the Athena Parthenos (Athena the Virgin), the massive statue stood almost 40 feet (12 m) tall. To the regret of later generations of art lovers, it did not survive ancient times. Fortunately, however, archaeologists discovered a few miniature versions that had been made as souvenirs for ancient tourists who visited Athens. Supplementing these are some images on surviving coins and a written description of the statue by the Greek traveler Pausanias, who saw it in the second century AD.

Based on this evidence, the sculpted goddess's left arm cradled a spear and shield, and her outstretched right hand held a 6-foot-high (1.8-m) statue of Nike, goddess of victory. The Athena Parthenos wore a magnificent helmet, which featured mythical creatures called

The statue of Athena Parthenos is depicted in a color engraving. The massive statue did not survive ancient times, but archaeologists have been able to create a likeness of the statue from various miniatures and other surviving evidence.

griffins on its sides, and on her chest was her impregnable breastplate, the aegis. To simulate the goddess's skin, Phidias used ivory, and he coated her tunic, which stretched to the floor, in sheets of gold.

While fashioning the giant statue, Phidias revealed to the Greeks of his day, as well as to people in future ages, that he had a playful sense of humor. But what began as a harmless in-joke soon backfired and led to the great artist's untimely death. In keeping with similar scenes carved on the temple's exterior, Phidias adorned the goddess's huge shield with "a relief of the battle of the Amazons," in Plutarch's words. A few Athenians became upset when they saw some of the details of the battle. Phidias had "carved a figure representing himself as a bald old man lifting up a stone with both hands." In addition, "he introduced a particularly fine likeness of Pericles fighting an Amazon."[32]

This incident afforded Pericles's political enemies a chance to discredit him by attacking his friend, Phidias. Someone prosecuted the sculptor, saying that placing his own likeness among the decorations was a display of disrespect for the city's divine patron. Poor Phidias ended up in jail, where a short time later he died.

Fortunately for him, his prosecution and death came two years after the Parthenon's completion in 432 BC. So he lived long enough to see perhaps his finest works become reality and to receive the accolades of most of his fellow citizens. These praises were destined to be repeated by witnesses to the building in one generation after another, right up to the present.

The reason for this enduring admiration is that the Parthenon's sculptures captured a vital essence of the human form and spirit. Even today, in their weathered and ruined state, these images speak powerfully to all who gaze on them. Regardless of the viewer's nationality or cultural background, he or she must recognize something universally human that reaches out and fills him or her with a sense of wonder. As Thomas Craven aptly put it, Phidias and the other artists with whom he worked "endowed marble with the effects of living tissue, living tissue that has been transformed into figures of indescribable serenity and nobility." The sculptors, according to Craven, went "from the mastery of movement and anatomy" to producing "ideal forms and faces, to the creation of figures, male and female, beyond those produced by nature." In an artistic achievement that remains unsurpassed, said Craven, the Parthenon's makers created works that "caress the eye with the glory of consummate carving, and set the standard of classic sculpture for all time."[33]

CHAPTER FOUR

Many Centuries of Worshippers

Following its completion in 432 BC, the Parthenon remained Athens's most famous building and one of its primary symbols for the nearly 830 years that it functioned as Athena's sacred house. During those long centuries, the temple and its divine occupant were central to worship in Greece's largest and most culturally splendid city. The Parthenon was also the leading tourist attraction in Athens, as well as in Greece overall. People came from far and wide to see the artistic masterpieces gracing the temple's entablature, and powerful men—from Greek kings to Roman emperors—used the building for their own purposes, hoping that some of its fame would rub off on them.

Facets of Athena's Personality

One fact that became evident to all those who visited ancient Athens was that despite the fame the Parthenon enjoyed, the building did not and could not stand alone. A hefty portion of its religious and cultural importance in Athens was tied in with the equally sacred structures surrounding it. The great temple was both integral to and dependent on the activities that took place in the Acropolis complex, just as Pericles and Phidias had intended from the start. Each part of the complex contributed important architectural and religious elements to a unified whole that stayed intact throughout antiquity and remains valid and crucial today.

First, in a general sense the Parthenon, Erechtheum, and Temple of Athena Nike were unified religiously speaking because they all paid homage to Athena. More specifically, however, each temple exemplified or embodied a different facet of Athena's personality and political-religious image. The particular aspect of the goddess that the Parthenon personified was her famed virginity.

In fact, the temple's very name reflected an image the Greeks believed Athena had fairly recently adopted. In many Greek homes a *parthenon* was a room in which a young woman, ideally a virgin, lived before she got married. This was the origin of the name Athena Parthenos—Athena the Virgin—that the Athenians gave the enormous cult image standing in the temple's cella. This feature of her personality reflected her feminine beauty and purity.

In contrast, the goddess's more aggressive character traits were explored in other sectors of the Acropolis. In the Temple of Athena Nike, she was portrayed as the victor, a protector of the city who had been instrumental in assuring the Athenian victory over the "barbarian" Persians at Marathon. Similarly, a towering bronze statue of Athena fashioned by Phidias stood on the hill not far from the entrance gate. Some 30 feet (9 m) tall, it was called the Athena Promachos, or Athena the Warrior Champion. According to Pausanias, Phidias obtained the bronze for the statue by melting down the numerous bronze weapons dropped by the fleeing Persians at Marathon. Also, Pausanias said, "the spear-tip and helmet-crest of this Athena can be seen as you come in by sea from Sounion,"[34] the southernmost tip of Attica, lying 43 miles (69 km) from the Acropolis!

Athena's Atypical House

The temples and other objects atop that hill were also united in an architectural-visual sense. For example, the sight of the looming Parthenon on the right as one stepped onto the Acropolis's summit was carefully balanced by placing the Erechtheum on the left. The Erechtheum was an Ionic structure. However, it was not a normal Ionic temple, but rather one of Greece's rare atypical temples. It had four porches, one each on its northern, southern, eastern, and western sides, and they formed a unique, purposely asymmetrical, split-level ground plan.

Another unusual touch was to use statues of women instead of columns as piers for the roof of the temple's southern porch. These six carved women, known as karyatids, gave that section of the Erechtheum its popular name—the Porch of the Maidens. (The six statues mounted on that porch today are reproductions. To save the originals from further deterioration, they now stand in assorted museums.)

The chief object resting inside the Erechtheum—an olivewood statue of Athena—was also crucial to maintaining the balance between that temple and the nearby Parthenon. This was because the statue and the garments draped around it were central to a major religious festival that involved both structures. One of Athens's most cherished myths claimed that during the Age of Heroes, the goddess had sent the statue hurtling down onto the Acropolis, as alluded to by Pausanias in his guidebook. The most sacred object in the Erechtheum, he said, was Athena's olivewood image. "Rumor says it fell from heaven. Whether this is true or not, I shall not argue about it." He went on to explain that the local priests kept an oil lamp burning year round inside. "It shines perpetually, night and day,"[35] he wrote. Presumably, this lamp was intended to provide the goddess with any illumination she might require when visiting the temple.

The Sacred Procession

The major religious festival that involved both the Parthenon and Erechtheum and centered on the deity honored by each was known as the Panathenaea. The word has been translated variously as "all the Athenians" or "rites of all Athenians." It had extremely archaic origins. The Athenians assumed it dated back to the Age of Heroes, today known to be the Bronze Age, but modern scholars think the festival developed later, sometime during the Dark Age.

Two separate myths claimed to tell how the festival came to be. In one, King Erechtheus established the Panathenaea to commemorate Athena's victory over a legendary giant. The other tale claimed that the early Athenian hero and king, Theseus, organized the festival after creating the Athenian nation. In that founding story, he unified Attica's formerly scattered towns and villages into a political whole, with the Acropolis as its central defensive site and governing place.

Whatever its actual origins may have been, the Panathenaea, at first strictly local in character, underwent an important restructuring

Statues of women, known as karyatids, did the work of columns—supporting the roof of the Erechtheum's southern porch. Reproductions of the karyatids (pictured) can be seen at the site today.

in 566 BC. From that time on, it was not only Athens's leading religious celebration, but also a Panhellenic event that attracted worshippers from many other Greek cities. Pericles's creation of the Parthenon, Erechtheum, and other shrines on the Acropolis in the century that followed further enhanced the festival's prestige and drawing power. It was held on a moderate scale each year and in its full-scale version, the Greater Panathenaea, every fourth year, traditionally in mid-August. In addition to worshipping Athena, the participants took part in lavish feasts and entertaining athletic and musical competitions.

The religious ceremonies, which remained at the festival's heart throughout the rest of ancient times, began with a proverbial bang in the form of a huge and magnificent parade in which thousands of citizens marched. This procession was very likely the one that Phidias and

PROSTITUTES IN THE PARTHENON

When Demetrius Poliorcetes seized Athens, he actually lived inside the Parthenon, where he committed numerous acts the Athenians viewed as outrageous—including consorting with prostitutes in Athena's sacred temple. In his biography of Demetrius, Plutarch recalled that he

> affected to call Athena his elder sister, and for this reason, if for no other, he ought at least to have shown her respect. But in fact he filled her temple with so many outrages committed against the persons of free-born youths and Athenian women that the place was considered unusually impure when he was content to live there with well-known prostitutes, such as Chrysis, Lamia, Demo, and Anticrya. For the sake of the city's good name I shall not enter into the details of Demetrius's other debaucheries [degrading behaviors].

Plutarch, "Life of Demetrius," in *The Age of Alexander: Nine Greek Lives* by Plutarch, trans. Ian Scott-Kilvert. New York: Penguin, 1973, pp. 354–55.

his assistants depicted in the Parthenon's Ionic frieze. Reflecting the fact that Athens was a democracy, in the era following the construction of the Parthenon and Erechtheum, the marchers represented all social classes and groups. In addition to male citizens, who could vote and hold public office, and female citizens, who lacked political rights, there were metics, Greeks from other states who lived and worked in Athens. Even some slaves marched in the procession. Old men wearing long, white robes bore olive branches in honor of the patron deity; women and children carried baskets and trays loaded with food, along with water jars; soldiers marched in full armor; musicians played a tune suitable for marching; and slaves proudly led the cows, goats, and other animals that would later be sacrificed to Athena.

As thousands of other Athenians watched, the parade began at the Dipylon gate, in Athens's northwest wall. It marked the starting point of the procession's time-honored route, known appropriately as the Panathenaic Way. From there the marchers made their way through the city's marketplace, called the Agora, and then headed for the Acropolis. They ascended the great stairway on the hill's western face and marched out onto the hill's summit. At that point, the Parthenon and Erechtheum were plainly visible up ahead.

The Offering of the Robe

The wide, open area situated between the two temples was dominated by a large marble altar. Before that sacred spot, the marchers halted and lined up to watch a series of ceremonies sacred to the patron goddess. The positioning of the altar halfway between the Parthenon and Erechtheum suggests that, as the city's two principal shrines devoted to Athena, both were crucial and equally important to the festival.

The exact nature and order of the ceremonies that ensued is uncertain. But some evidence suggests that the first one was the offering of a sacred robe to Athena. Known as the *peplos*, it had been made some months before by two girls between the ages of seven and eleven (at which point, it was assumed, they were virgins like the goddess). Each year two new girls were given this honor because a fresh robe was required for each annual Panathenaea.

Specially chosen marchers carried the peplos in the parade, and when that stream of worshippers reached the area lying between the Parthenon and Erechtheum, someone brought the robe forward. With due reverence, he or she carried it to a waiting man and boy, who, like all those who touched the peplos, had been specially chosen for the occasion. The man and boy then proceeded to fold the garment while everyone else looked on.

Historians know about the folding ceremony because it was depicted by the Parthenon's sculptors in a section of the Ionic frieze. "From the thickness of the already-folded mass of cloth," New York University scholar Evelyn B. Harrison states, "we can guess that the two figures here are making the last fold. The man holds up the cloth in his two hands with part of it flapped over." Meanwhile, she says, "the child is smoothing out the wrinkles and helping to bring the corners together."[36]

The consensus of modern experts is that this act of folding the peplos signified that it had been officially offered to the goddess. Later, in separate ceremonies, people draped the robe around her olive-wood statue inside the Erechtheum after removing the one from the festival held the year before.

Other Panathenaic Ceremonies

After the folding ceremony was completed, a succession of animal sacrifices was held at the grand altar lying between the two temples.

Each Panathenaea witnessed the ritual slaughter of one hundred cows and numerous sheep and other animals. Some of the beasts were raised in Attica, while others came from neighboring city-states.

Abiding by traditions dating back an unknown number of centuries, each animal sacrifice followed a series of set rituals. Archaeologist Roy A. Adkins describes them, beginning with the sprinkling of water over the creature to be sacrificed, called the victim. Next, he says,

> unground barleycorn was sprinkled over the victim, altar, and possibly the participants. Hair was cut from the victim's head and burned on the altar. The victim was then killed with a blow from an ax, and its throat was cut. Blood was collected in a bowl and splashed on the altar. The animal was then butchered, and the portion selected for the god was burned on the altar (apparently usually thigh bones wrapped in fat—worthless as food), while wine was simultaneously poured into the flames. The entrails were cooked separately and tasted first, then the remaining meat was cooked and eaten by the participants in a sacrificial feast.[37]

These large-scale sacrifices and feasts took place in the shadow of the Parthenon. After the strictly religious activities were over, they were followed by a few days that were devoted to the festival's athletic and musical contests. It is uncertain exactly where they were held. But some evidence implies that the ceremony in which the awards were handed out took place beside or in front of the Parthenon. Modern experts think it likely that Athens's leaders chose this spot in order to show off the building. Hundreds, if not thousands, of Greeks from other cities attended the Panathenaic contests. Distributing the prizes for their winners before the temple's breathtaking façade was an opportunity to remind foreigners of the purported superiority of Athenian culture.

Athens in Decline

The Athenians maintained the rituals associated with their greatest religious festival for many centuries after the Periclean Age. The considerable power and prestige their city enjoyed in that era did not last nearly as long, however. As time went on, Athens steadily declined in wealth, influence, and esteem. The structures adorning the Acropolis remained marvels to behold, but the city itself retained little of its former authority and glory.

The first major misfortune Athens suffered was losing the Peloponnesian War. Lasting from 431 to 404 BC, it pitted the city-state and its allies against Sparta and its allies. The conflict exhausted nearly all involved and ended with Athens's unconditional surrender. As if this was not tragic enough, the Greeks had failed to learn the lesson that disunity was harmful to them. The Athenians and their neighbors continued to oppose one another in smaller conflicts, causing them to grow collectively weaker.

The result was hardship for all. In the 330s BC, Macedonia, a kingdom occupying Greece's northernmost sector, was able to take full advantage of the leading city-states' increasing disunity and weakness. First King Philip II, and then his son, Alexander III (later called "the Great") exerted control over the other Greeks. Alexander led them in the successful conquest of their former enemy, Persia, but then he suddenly died in 323 BC just shy of his thirty-third birthday. In the years that followed, his leading generals and some of their sons came to death grips over control of his enormous empire.

During these devastating wars, one of those sons, the brilliant but arrogant Demetrius Poliorcetes, seized Athens. He insulted and outraged the local citizenry by making the Parthenon his personal quarters and cavorting with prostitutes there. A few years later, in 295 BC, another Greek military strongman stripped the gold sheets from

A colored engraving depicts a cow being sacrificed in ancient Greece. Animal sacrifices took place at the grand altar between the Parthenon and the Erechtheum.

the giant statue in the temple's cella and melted down the metal to make new coins.

Over time more infighting among the Greeks occurred and eventually made them vulnerable to conquest by outsiders. This time it was the Romans, the masters of the Italian Peninsula, who managed to overwhelm most of the Greek city-states and kingdoms by 146 BC. A majority of Romans came to admire Greek culture, and the Parthenon and other temples on the Acropolis impressed them greatly. Yet some Roman leaders thoughtlessly misused these structures. In 37 BC, for example, the famous military general Mark Antony mirrored Demetrius's misdeeds by engaging in nightly orgies inside the Parthenon.

THE PARTHENON'S "SHAMEFUL SECRET"

Little information about any visits the Roman emperors made to the Parthenon has survived. But thanks to the brilliant detective work of a young American scholar named Eugene Andrews, a fascinating incident involving one emperor and the Parthenon was revealed. A graduate of Cornell University, Andrews attended a lecture in Athens in 1895. The scholar giving the talk pointed out the existence of some faint, very odd scrapes just beneath the metopes on one side of the structure. Up to that time, no one had been able to figure out what had caused the marks. Accepting the challenge, Andrews obtained a rope ladder, climbed up to the metopes, and methodically took molds of the scrapes using soft, wet paper. He discovered that they had been caused by large letters that had once been attached to the entablature, spelling out a message. Deciphering the words, he found that they formed a greeting from the Athenians to Emperor Nero, who visited the city in AD 61. Because of Nero's reputation for corruption and cruelty, Andrews was unhappy that the temple had been defaced to honor him. "I felt no elation," Andrews later remarked, "at having torn from the Parthenon its shameful secret."

Quoted in Kevin K. Carroll, *The Parthenon Inscription*. Durham, NC: Duke University Press, 1982, p. 7.

The Worst Insult Yet

As the ancient centuries wore on, the Acropolis and Parthenon suffered further indignities. One of the worst occurred in the early 400s AD, when Roman leaders had both of Phidias's imposing statues, the Athena Parthenos and Athena Promachos, removed from Athens. They were taken to Rome's new eastern capital, Constantinople. In the decades that followed, both of these sculptural masterpieces vanished.

In the year 529 Athens suffered the worst insult yet to the memory of its former greatness. The eastern Roman emperor Justinian closed the city's widely respected schools of philosophy, after which few outsiders visited anymore. Soon Athens was little more than a small, half-forgotten village on Europe's southeastern flank. For the Parthenon, which still stood silently on the central hill, its thousand-year-long existence in the ancient world was over. But many medieval and modern centuries loomed ahead, during which it would undergo changes far more dramatic than any it had so far endured.

CHAPTER FIVE

Proud and Magnificent in Ruin

nlike many other ancient structures, during medieval times the Parthenon did not rapidly fall into ruin as a result of neglect, vandalism, and other factors. This was mainly because the various groups that controlled Greece over the centuries admired its beauty and solid construction and decided to use it for their own purposes. Among the roles it played were those of Christian church and Muslim mosque. Its diverse occupiers did make a few minor alterations in its exterior and interior. But most aspects of the original building survived intact for more than twenty-one centuries. Not until the monstrous explosion of 1687, at the sunrise of the modern era, was it suddenly and catastrophically transformed into a vacant ruin.

As it turned out, even in an awful state of disrepair the Parthenon could not be ignored. The modern world rediscovered it, scurried to save it from utter oblivion, and gave it a vital new task to fulfill. This was to act as a timeless and inspiring monument to the artistic splendor and cultural accomplishments of the ancient Greeks, in large degree Western society's founders.

From Cathedral to Mosque to Ruin

Long before that modern role for the Parthenon commenced, however, it endured a long medieval interlude as a Christian church. It is unclear exactly when a group of monks took control of the abandoned structure, but modern experts think it was sometime in the mid- to late 500s. What had been the refuge of the chaste Athena Parthenos was eventually rededicated to another sacred female virgin—Parthenos Maria, also known as Mary the mother of Jesus.

Renamed first the Church of Agia Sophia, then later the cathedral of Our Lady of Athens, and later still the cathedral of Notre Dame d'Athenes, the Parthenon required a few structural changes to qualify it as a Christian house of worship. One was to cut a new door in the west wall, since Christian custom demanded that a church be entered from the west. The monks also added a Christian altar on the inside, so that priests could conduct services where Phidias's towering statue of Athena had once stood. Finally, the Christians painted a mural of the biblical Last Judgment on one of the cella's walls. Turkish traveler and writer Evliya Celebi saw what was left of the image when he visited the Parthenon in the 1640s. According to his description, it showed "demons, devils, wild beasts, and sorceresses, and angels, and dragons, and antiChrists, and Cyclopes [one-eyed monsters], and creatures with a thousand shapes, and crocodiles, and elephants, and giraffes, and owls, and centipedes."[38]

> **WORDS IN CONTEXT**
> minaret
> *A tall, slender tower customarily attached to an Islamic mosque.*

The Parthenon's years of Christian service ended in the 1450s, when the Turks seized Athens and turned the structure into a mosque. The Muslims made their own alterations, the most extensive of which was the addition of a minaret. A tall spire, it had a platform at the top where the muezzin called the faithful to prayer several times a day. (During this same period the local Turkish leader used the Erechtheum as living quarters for the women of his harem.) Surrounded by small houses the Turks had erected on the Acropolis, the Parthenon was still a mosque in 1687, when the violent explosion set off by a Venetian cannonball destroyed large sections of it.

(Opposite page) Sometime in the mid- to late 500s, experts believe, the Parthenon was sanctified as a Christian church and rededicated to Mary, the mother of Jesus. It served in this capacity for hundreds of years.

A Passionate Nostalgia

For a while, those who looked on the blasted-out shell of the formerly imposing temple, church, and mosque assumed its usefulness was at an end. Its shattered remnants would simply crumble and disappear over time, they imagined. But they were wrong. In the decades that followed the disaster, the Parthenon became known to the residents of England, France, Germany, the United States, and other Western nations. Increasingly, its deteriorating walls, columns, and entablature attracted the attention of architects, painters, scholars, poets, and others who had acquired a fascination for the ancient Greeks.

Gripped by a passionate nostalgia for Greece's lost cultural glories, those Westerners began to visit Athens. Climbing the same steps that centuries before had led the Panathenaea's marchers to the Acropolis's summit, they marveled at the ruins of what they believed had been exceedingly noble, even heroic human works. From the mid-1700s on, ardent and adoring written descriptions of the Parthenon began to appear in European and American articles, poems, and books. "Nothing in all Greece, nor even the whole world, was equal to the magnificence of this temple,"[39] England's Earl of Sandwich stated after his late-eighteenth-century sojourn in Athens. "What a superb monument!" South American diplomat Francisco de Miranda said during the same period. "Nothing I have seen so far deserves to be compared with it!"[40] Following his arrival in Athens in 1809, the English baron and writer John Hobhouse remarked that even in its advanced state of ruin, the Parthenon "cannot fail to fill the mind of the most indifferent spectator with sentiments of astonishment and awe."[41]

Such romantic appreciation for the Parthenon's form and beauty also called attention to the visual nobility and attractiveness of the Doric architectural style. European and American architects eagerly began to replicate its features in modern structures ranging from courthouses and banks to government buildings and mansions of the rich. The Parthenon's contours and architectural aspects proved especially popular in the United States, where the Greek Revival style became the rage. English architect Benjamin Latrobe's completion of the Bank of Pennsylvania in 1801 was followed by the erection of Greek-style buildings in numerous American cities and towns. Outstanding examples included the Second Bank of the United States in Philadelphia, the Custom House of Wall Street in New York City, and the Boston Customs House—all built before 1850.

The Elgin Marbles

Even as the Parthenon and its architectural form excited Western architects and inspired them to copy Greek Doric temples, some Westerners exploited the once great structure in more selfish and destructive ways. A number of private art enthusiasts and/or collectors thought nothing of vandalizing the Parthenon and the other buildings on the Acropolis. Sometimes seeking the permission of local Turkish authorities and other times not, they sliced, drilled, hacked, and otherwise detached large pieces of these edifices and carted them away to other countries.

Probably the best-known example was that of a British nobleman—Thomas Bruce, Seventh Earl of Elgin, better known as Lord Elgin. Between 1801 and 1812, he hired laborers who stripped away 247 feet (75 m), or close to half, of the Parthenon's Ionic frieze. He also took several large statues from the temple's metopes and pediments. Elgin sold these priceless antiquities for a profit, but eventually they ended up in London's British Museum.

Historians and other scholars and writers saw the acquisition of the so-called Elgin Marbles as both robbery and a disfigurement of precious ancient monuments. Since that time, many people, along with Greek officials, have requested that Britain return the Elgin Marbles. To date, however, they remain on display in London.

AMERICA'S PARTHENON

In addition to banks and other buildings whose architecture is based on the Parthenon and other ancient Doric temples, several cities around the globe have created structures intended as specific replicas of the Parthenon. The most structurally accurate and visually stunning version is the one erected in 1897 for the Tennessee Centennial Exposition in Nashville, the so-called Athens of the South. Initially, the structure was supposed to be dismantled after the exposition was over. But it was so popular that the city decided to keep it intact. Workers rebuilt it between 1925 and 1931, replacing its original wood, brick, and plaster with stronger and longer-lasting concrete. They also added copies of the Ionic frieze made from direct casts taken from the originals in London's British Museum and Athens's Acropolis Museum. A second renovation took place in 1988 at a cost of $2 million. The Nashville Parthenon, which now serves as a museum, still draws large numbers of tourists from around the world. Many come to see the huge replica of Phidias's Athena Parthenos that Nashville sculptor Alan LeQuire fashioned for the cella in 1990. Others are drawn to colorful productions of ancient Greek plays staged there each summer.

Rescue Efforts Begin

During the same years that many Westerners were condemning Elgin's exploits in Greece, they also expressed growing concerns that the Parthenon, Erechtheum, and numerous other priceless ancient Greek structures were crumbling rapidly. Hobhouse painted a bleak picture of the remains of the Parthenon's interior, saying, "Within the cella of the temple, all is desolation and ruin. The shafts of columns, fragments of the entablatures, and of the beams of the roof, are scattered about on every side, but especially in the north side of the area, where there are vast piles of marble."[42] Both Hobhouse and his friend and traveling companion, English poet Lord Byron, warned that the Parthenon and its sister monuments might be lost forever unless someone launched major efforts to save them.

Such rescue attempts were not possible, however, because the Turks still controlled Greece. They lacked both an understanding of and an interest in restoring and safeguarding ancient ruins, so they refused to permit such activities. Fortunately for art lovers around the world, not to mention Greece itself, the Greeks fought a war for independence in the 1820s and eventually drove the Turks out. In March 1833 Turkish soldiers who were holding the Acropolis against a siege

Metal scaffolding covers portions of the Parthenon during a modern reconstruction project. The project, which is ongoing, involves a careful restoration of hundreds of building fragments found at the site.

by Greek freedom fighters surrendered. Thereafter, for the first time in history, all the inhabitants of the Greek mainland and nearby islands came together to form a single nation called Greece.

One of the first things the government of the newly independent Greece did was to grant permission for archaeologists and other experts to begin rescuing Athens's crumbling antiquities. One important priority was to clear away the houses, fortifications, and other medieval and modern structures that had accumulated atop the Acropolis over the previous few centuries. When this enormous project was at last completed, the Greek official in charge of it proudly stated, "Thus does Greece deliver the Acropolis back to the civilized world, cleansed of all barbaric additions."[43]

Meanwhile, even as workers were removing those unwanted additions, teams of trained experts began restoring the Parthenon and other ancient features of the Acropolis. The first intensive effort of this kind was that of Greek excavator Kyriakos Pittakis in the early 1840s. Similar endeavors took place in 1872, under the direction of Greek architect Panayis Kalkos, and in 1899–1902 and 1922–1933, led by Greek civil engineer Nikolaos Balanos.

Balanos's efforts proved to be both a help and a hindrance. On the positive side, he restored the building's side colonnades, large parts of which had been knocked down by the 1687 explosion. This made the shattered structure look much more whole and visually impressive. However, Balanos committed some serious mistakes as well, as Mary Beard explains:

First, he made very little attempt to replace blocks in their original position. Any column drum would do if it fitted well enough where he wanted it. In this sense, his work was nothing like an accurate reconstruction, but rather a plausible fiction made out of the material he had at hand. Even more critical, though, was his use of iron rods and clamps throughout the building, inside the ancient marble blocks. In due course, this iron oxidized and expanded, splitting open the very masonry it was supposed to be holding in place. Balanos's Parthenon was literally a time-bomb waiting to burst apart.[44]

Not a Single Straight Line

Happily for all modern philhellenes (lovers of Greek culture), later twentieth-century experts recognized the damage Balanos had done and set out to correct his errors. In 1975 the Greek government established the Committee for the Preservation of the Acropolis Monuments, made up of teams of top-notch archaeologists, architects, engineers, and chemists. Greek architect Manolis Korres initially headed the committee. He ordered the creation of a careful, detailed study of the entire Acropolis. This included a painstaking search that turned up nearly one thousand pieces of the Parthenon that earlier restorers had missed.

With a new, systematic, scientifically sound plan in hand, in 1986 a small army of specially trained workers sheathed the Parthenon in modern metal scaffolding and began literally to take the building apart. As time went on, they started to put it back together again, fragment by fragment, this time with all the pieces in the right places. This enormous project is still ongoing and not expected to be finished until 2020.

Wherever possible, the current restorers have been particularly careful to maintain the integrity of a large number of extremely subtle construction tricks the original builders employed. Modern architects call them "refinements." Earlier archaeologists and engineers who attempted to restore the Parthenon noticed something that at the time seemed strange. Namely, there was not a single truly straight line in the building. Instead, it had been purposely designed with dozens of small, yet crucial visual deceptions intended to enhance its look. The first modern expert to notice and measure these refinements was British architect Francis C. Penrose. "No two neighboring capitals correspond in size," he pointed out. In addition,

the diameters of columns are unequal, inter-columnar spaces are irregular, the metope spaces are of varying width, none of the apparently vertical lines are true perpendiculars, the columns all lean towards the center of the building, as do the side walls, and antae [pillars lining the entrances] at the angles lean forward, the architrave and frieze lean backward, the main horizontal lines of construction are in curves which rise in vertical planes to the center of each side, and these curves do not form parallels.[45]

The reasons for incorporating these refinements are now understood. With the benefit of knowledge gained from centuries of Greek

⬡ ANCIENT TOOLS BETTER THAN TODAY'S?

A number of modern experts have questioned how the Parthenon's builders managed to complete such a large and complex building in only a little more than a decade without the benefit of modern motor-driven lifting devices. As scholar Evan Hadingham explains, one possibility is that the handheld tools used by the Athenian masons were superior to their modern counterparts.

> After analyzing marks left on the marble surfaces, [some archaeologists are] convinced that centuries of metallurgical experimentation enabled the ancient Athenians to create chisels and axes that were sharper and more durable than those available today. The idea is not unprecedented. Modern metallurgists have only recently figured out the secrets of the traditional samurai sword, which Japanese sword-smiths endowed with unrivaled sharpness and strength by regulating the amount of carbon in the steel and the temperature during forging and cooling. [Similarly] the ancient masons, with their superior tools, could carve marble at more than double the rate of today's craftsmen. And the Parthenon's original laborers had the benefit of experience, drawing on a century and a half of temple-building know-how.

Evan Hadingham, "Unlocking the Mysteries of the Parthenon," Smithsonian, February 2008. www.smithsonianmag.com.

temple building, Ictinus and his associates realized that in large buildings perfectly straight lines frequently do not appear straight to the eye. Long horizontal bases or cornices can seem to sag a bit

in the middle, for example. Also, when an absolutely straight vertical column is seen against the sky, its middle part can deceivingly look thinner than its upper and lower sections. To compensate for this effect, the Parthenon's builders added a very slight swelling, or outward curvature, of the middles of the column shafts. This visual trick is called entasis.

This and the other refinements were executed with phenomenal exactness. Despite the temple's immense size—hundreds of feet long and nearly seven stories high—the overall margin of error of the proportions and refinements was less than a quarter of an inch (6 mm), thinner than a person's eyebrow. This is one of the primary reasons that architects often call the Parthenon the most perfect structure ever erected.

Humanity's Universal Judgment

As the overseers and skilled construction workers of the Parthenon's massive new facelift labor to keep these delicate proportions intact, they caution the public that their goal is not to make it look new and unscathed, as it appeared in 432 BC. Instead, their aim is to stop its deterioration, make it structurally stable, and preserve it for future generations. This is imperative, historians, artists, and architects say, because it is unarguably a true wonder of both the ancient and modern worlds.

In this respect, the Parthenon stunningly fulfills the prophecy made during Athens's golden age by the man who more than anyone else made the building possible. Standing before his countrymen in the recently completed temple's mighty shadow, Pericles made a bold prediction. "Future ages will look on our achievements with wonder," he said, "as the age we live in wonders at us now."[46]

The speaker could not have known that more than twenty-four centuries later, a man who loved Athens no less than he did would stand in nearly the same spot and confirm the correctness of those insightful words. In 1912 the popular nineteenth-century Irish scholar and ardent philhellene John Pentland Mahaffy visited Greece. On Easter Day he made his way through Athens's narrow, winding streets and eagerly climbed the Acropolis's western stairway, its marble steps now noticeably worn by the tread of countless feet over innumerable ages.

A timeless edifice, the Parthenon still inspires awe and wonder. It recalls a time of grand achievements and a culture unparalleled in the ancient world.

Reaching the hill's summit, Mahaffy gazed in awe at the Parthenon's cracked yet noble visage and felt tears of joy well up in his eyes. Not long afterward, he found some paper and scribbled, "There is no ruin, all the world over, which combines so much striking beauty [with] so vast a volume of history [and] so great a pageant of immortal memories." Then, with a flourish, he composed a phrase destined to be repeated often in the years to come, a handful of words that have proved to be humanity's universal judgment of that timeless edifice. "All the Old World's culture culminated in Greece," he declared, "all Greece in Athens, all Athens in its Acropolis, and all the Acropolis in the Parthenon."[47]

SOURCE NOTES

Introduction: An "Extraordinary Flowering of the Human Spirit"

1. Quoted in Peter Green, *The Parthenon*. New York: Newsweek, Inc., Book Division, 1973, p. 144.
2. Edward Dodwell, *A Classical and Topographical Tour Through Greece During the Years 1801, 1805, and 1806*, vol. 1. London: Rockwell and Martin, 1819, pp. 324–25.
3. Plutarch, "Life of Pericles," in *The Rise and Fall of Athens: Nine Greek Lives* by Plutarch, trans. Ian Scott-Kilvert. New York: Penguin, 2011, p. 178.
4. Quoted in Charles Mitchell, "History, Archaeological Analysis, and Criticism," in *The Parthenon*, ed. Vincent J. Bruno. New York: Norton, 1974, p. 113.
5. Dodwell, *A Classical and Topographical Tour Through Greece During the Years 1801, 1805, and 1806*, vol. 1, p. 321.
6. Quoted in Mary Beard, *The Parthenon*. Cambridge, MA: Harvard University Press, 2010, p. 4.
7. Thomas Craven, *The Pocket Book of Greek Art*. New York: Pocket, 1950, pp. 45, 48.
8. Plutarch, *Life of Pericles*, p. 179.
9. Green, *The Parthenon*, p. 134.

Chapter One: The Rise of the Greek Temple

10. James Fenimore Cooper, *Home as Found*. New York: Townsend, 1860, p. 22.
11. C.M. Bowra, *The Greek Experience*. New York: Barnes and Noble, 1996, p. 69.
12. Craven, *The Pocket Book of Greek Art*, p. 44.
13. Hesiod, *Theogony*, excerpted in *Classical Gods and Heroes: Myths as Told by the Ancient Authors*, ed. and trans. Rhoda A. Hendricks. New York: Morrow Quill, 1974, pp. 38–39.

14. John A. Crow, *Greece: The Magic Spring*. New York: Harper & Row, 1970, p. 128.

Chapter Two: The Planning and Structural Phases

15. Quoted in Lycurgus, *Against Leokrates*, in *Minor Attic Orators*, vol. 2, trans. J.O. Burtt. Cambridge, MA: Harvard University Press, 1957, p. 73.
16. Quoted in Thucydides, *The Peloponnesian War*, published as *The Landmark Thucydides: A Comprehensive Guide to the Peloponnesian War*, trans. Richard Crawley. New York: Simon & Schuster, 1996, p. 115.
17. Plutarch, "Life of Pericles," p. 179.
18. Green, *The Parthenon*, p. 71.
19. Plutarch, "Life of Pericles," pp. 178–79.
20. Green, *The Parthenon*, p. 77.
21. Lesley Adkins and Roy A. Adkins, *Handbook to Life in Ancient Greece*. New York: Facts On File, 2005, p. 228.
22. Plutarch, "Life of Pericles," p. 178.

Chapter Three: Decorations to Please the Gods

23. Beard, *The Parthenon*, p. 141.
24. John Miliadis, *The Acropolis*. Athens: Pechlivanidis, p. 44.
25. Vincent J. Bruno, "The Parthenon and the Theory of Classical Form," in Bruno, *The Parthenon*, pp. 96–97.
26. Nigel Spivey, *Greek Art*. London: Phaidon, 1997, pp. 221, 224.
27. Spivey, *Greek Art*, p. 250.
28. A.W. Lawrence, *Greek Architecture*, rev. ed. R.A. Tomlinson. New Haven: Yale University Press, 1996, p. 73.
29. John Boardman, *The Parthenon and Its Sculptures*. Austin: University of Texas, 1985, p. 34.
30. Boardman, *The Parthenon and Its Sculptures*, pp. 34–35.
31. Miliadis, *The Acropolis*, p. 47.
32. Plutarch, "Life of Pericles," p. 198.
33. Craven, *Greek Art*, pp. 36–37 and plate 14.

Chapter Four: Many Centuries of Worshippers

34. Pausanias, *Guide to Greece,* vol. 1, trans. Peter Levi. New York: Penguin, 1984, pp. 79–80.

35. Pausanias, *Guide to Greece,* vol. 1, p. 75.

36. Evelyn B. Harrison, "The Web of History: A Conservative Reading of the Parthenon Frieze," in *Worshipping Athena: Panathenaia and Parthenon,* ed. Jenifer Neils. Madison: University of Wisconsin Press, 1996, p. 202.

37. Adkins and Adkins, *Handbook to Life in Ancient Greece,* pp. 345–46.

Chapter Five: Proud and Magnificent in Ruin

38. Quoted in Richard Stoneman, *A Traveler's History of Athens.* Northhampton, MA: Interlink, 2004, p. 209.

39. Quoted in Panayotis Tournikiotis, ed., *The Parthenon and Its Impact in Modern Times.* New York: Abrams, 1996, p. 34.

40. Quoted in Tournikiotis, *The Parthenon and Its Impact in Modern Times,* p. 34.

41. Quoted in Green, *The Parthenon,* p. 147.

42. John Hobhouse, *Journey Through Albania and Other Provinces of Turkey in Europe and Asia, to Constantinople, During the Years 1809 and 1810,* vol. 1. Philadelphia: Carey and Son, 1817, p. 283.

43. Quoted in Nicholas Reeves and Dyfri Williams, "The Parthenon in Ruins," *British Museum Magazine,* Spring/Summer 2007. www.nicholasreeves.com.

44. Beard, *The Parthenon,* p. 113.

45. Francis C. Penrose, *An Investigation of the Principles of Athenian Architecture.* London: Nicol, 1851, p. 29.

46. Quoted in Thucydides, *The Peloponnesian War.* Passage translated by Don Nardo.

47. John Pentland Mahaffy, *Rambles and Studies in Greece.* New York: Macmillan, 1913, p. 78.

FACTS ABOUT THE PARTHENON

The Builders
- The chief sculptor and overall artistic director was Phidias, widely viewed as the greatest sculptor of ancient times.
- The principal architect was Ictinus.

Construction Materials
- The marble used came from Mount Pentelicon, situated 10 miles (16 km) from Athens's urban center.
- The temple used about 30,000 tons (27,215 metric tons) of Pentelic marble.
- A reported 2,500 pounds (1,134 kg) of pure gold was used in the creation of the huge statue in the cella.

Weight
- Each of the building's columns weighed approximately 91 tons (82.5 metric tons).
- The entire pteron weighed about 4,368 tons (3,962 metric tons).
- The roof weighed roughly 3,000 tons (2,720 metric tons).

Size
- The overall length of the temple was 228 feet (69 m).
- The building's width was 101 feet (31 m).
- The structure was 65 feet (20 m) high.
- The Ionic frieze was 524 feet (160 m) long.
- The cella was 108 feet (33 m) long, 62 feet (19 m) wide, and 43 feet (13 m) high.

- The giant statue of Athena inside the cella was 40 or so feet (12 m) tall.

Other Features

- The temple featured 188 mutules, each with 18 guttae.
- The overall margin of error for the refinements was less than 0.25 inches (6 mm).
- The temple's total cost was about 30 million drachmas.

FOR FURTHER RESEARCH

Books

Lesley Adkins and Roy A. Adkins, *Handbook to Life in Ancient Greece*. New York: Facts On File, 2005.

Mary Beard, *The Parthenon*. Cambridge, MA: Harvard University Press, 2010.

Carl Bluemel, *Greek Sculptors at Work*. London: Phaidon, 1969.

Michael Grant, *The Rise of the Greeks*. New York: Macmillan, 2001.

Peter Green, *The Shadow of the Parthenon*. Berkeley: University of California Press, 2008.

Herodotus, *The Histories*. Translated by Aubrey de Sélincourt. New York: Penguin, 2003.

Ian Jenkins, *Explore the Parthenon*. London: British Museum, 2009.

A.W. Lawrence, *Greek Architecture*, rev. ed. (R.A. Tomlinson. New Haven: Yale University Press), 1996.

Jenifer Neils, ed., *Worshipping Athena: Panathenaia and Parthenon*. Madison: University of Wisconsin Press, 1996.

Jenifer Neils, *The Parthenon Frieze*. New York: Cambridge University Press, 2006.

Pausanias, *Guide to Greece*. 2 vols. Translated by Peter Levi. New York: Penguin, 1988.

John G. Pedley, *Greek Art and Archaeology*. Rancho Cordova, CA: Pearson, 2011.

Plutarch, *Parallel Lives*. Excerpted in *The Rise and Fall of Athens: Nine Greek Lives* by Plutarch. Translated by Ian Scott-Kilvert. New York: Penguin, 2011.

Sarah B. Pomeroy et al. *Ancient Greece: A Political, Social, and Cultural History*. New York: Oxford University Press, 2011.

Tony Spawforth, *The Complete Greek Temples*. London: Thames and Hudson, 2006.

R.A. Tomlinson, *Greek Architecture*. Dulles, VA: Bristol Classical, 2009.

Panayotis Tournikiotis, ed., *The Parthenon and Its Impact in Modern Times*. New York: Abrams, 1996.

R.E. Wycherley, *The Stones of Athens*. Princeton, NJ: Princeton University Press, 1992.

Websites

Acropolis Architecture, Ancient-Greece.org (www.ancient-greece .org/architecture/acropolis-arch.html). Provides descriptions of the various temples and other structures associated with the Acropolis, including the Parthenon. Click on the appropriate link and find both a written description and pictures of some of the structures in question.

Conservancy for the Parthenon and Centennial Park (www.conser vancyonline.com/pages/parthenon.htm). Tells about the magnificent full-scale replica of the Parthenon standing in Nashville, Tennessee. Click on the links to learn more, including how and when to visit.

The Greeks: Crucible of Civilization, PBS (www.pbs.org/empires /thegreeks). This excellent online resource based on the acclaimed PBS show includes not only much information about ancient Greek history and culture, but also a virtual tour of the Acropolis and Parthenon.

Parthenon: Gallery of Images, State University of New York, Oneonta College (http://employees.oneonta.edu/farberas/arth/AR TH209/Parthenon_gallery.html). Includes a large collection of attractive photos, diagrams, grounds plans, and other images relating to the Parthenon and the Acropolis.

Parthenon, Great Buildings Online (www.greatbuildings.com /buildings/The_Parthenon.html). This site provided by the prestigious Great Buildings Online staff is one of the better ones on the Internet about this iconic structure.

Parthenon, Michael Lahanas (www.mlahanas.de/Greeks/Arts/Par thenon.htm). This site contains some excellent color drawings and schematics of the Parthenon.

"Secrets of the Parthenon," *NOVA* (www.pbs.org/wgbh/nova/an cient/secrets-parthenon.html). Click on "watch the program" and enjoy this beautifully produced television production introducing the Parthenon's wonders.

INDEX

PICTURE CREDITS

Cover: Thinkstock Images

Maury Aaseng: 11, 40

Akg-images/Rabatti-Domingie/Newscom: 34

© Bettmann/Corbis: 25

© Stefano Bianchetti/Corbis: 7, 67

© Wolfgang Kaehler/Corbis: 46

© Ali Meter/Corbis: 19

© National Geographic Society/Corbis; 29

Thinkstock Images: 4, 5, 15, 61, 72, 76, 81

Athena Parthenos, statue from the Parthenon, Athens (colour engraving), French School, (19th century)/Bibliotheque des Arts Decoratifs, Paris, France/Archives Charmet/The Bridgeman Art Library: 55

ABOUT THE AUTHOR

Historian Don Nardo is best known for his books for young people about the ancient and medieval worlds. These include histories of ancient Greece, Rome, Egypt, Mesopotamia, and medieval Europe, along with studies of ancient and medieval art and architecture, including Mesopotamian cities and literature, Egyptian sculpture and monuments, Greek temples, Roman amphitheaters and circuses, and medieval castles, sculpture, and painting. Nardo also composes and arranges orchestral music. He lives with his wife, Christine, in Massachusetts.